I0483710

Emerging Issues and Technologies for ERP Systems

Class of Enterprise Systems Integration 2011/2012

School of Computing and Mathematics

University of Derby

Derby, UK

Foreword

This edited book represents the contributions of the final year 2011-12 Class studying 'Enterprise Systems Integration' as part of an undergraduate honours degree at the University of Derby.

Students in the class conducted a number of investigations into emerging topics within the subject area of Enterprise Resource Planning systems, and used the processes of research to collaboratively produce this publication.

The School of Computing and Mathematics enjoys a rich and diverse set of students and staff, who engage in many different and exciting forms of enquiry. This publication is but one example of the innovative activity that takes place within our School.

Knowledge creation through research is a key aspect of the learning journey in the School of Computing and Mathematics. We pride ourselves on the fact that our curriculum delivery facilitates 'students as producers'; the production of new knowledge and insight is a fundamental requirement for the ever more demanding employment market.

This edited book is but one example of how students in the School of Computing and Mathematics go further in their studies and accomplish more.

I am sure that you will join me in celebrating the achievement of our students.

Dr Richard Hill
Head of Subject, Computing and Mathematics
University of Derby

Table of Contents

Data quality problems when implementing an ERP system

Alaa Ameen

Information Technology

University of Derby

Derby, UK

100241063@unimail.derby.ac.uk

Abstract— Data quality issues have proofed to have huge impact on an organization's ERP system performance. Thus, it is crucial to gain knowledge about DQ issues to ensure success of ERP implementations .This research defines data quality in the context of ERP, identifies data quality issues, and discusses critical successes factors impacting data quality in ERP, in addition to using a case study which included SAP as an ERP system.

Introduction

ERP projects have often been found to be complex and risky to implement in business enterprises. For enterprises who want to implement an ERP system it is critical to understand data quality issues, enterprises should gain knowledge of the critical success factors that impacts data quality during the implementation process of an ERP. A lot of researchers were interested in data quality issues such as [4] who decided to study the importance of resolving DQ issues in ERP implementations, on other hand [9] thought about DQ methods based on ERP management principles, others have studied DQ in ERP systems and conducted an analysis about the causes of data quality problems.

Data quality also known as information quality and it is identified as data or information that is being used by the enterprise's employees [11]. According to [1] the identified data quality elements are completeness, consistency, timeliness and accuracy. Data quality problems and issues became more important to large enterprises to achieve their goals, gain advantage over different competitors, and continue to live in today's global economy thus, quality of data is important for a business to succeed, however not many organizations tend to take actions to solve DQ issues. [2].This paper discusses DQ issues and methodology and findings of the research knowing that SAP is used as an example of an ERP.

Background

There are a number of factors that have an impact on data quality in ERP systems and these factors are similar to those related to information systems in general. Many studies has been conducted to focus on the critical success factors in DQ management such as just in time and total quality

management .Other data quality researchers has addressed the critical key steps for data quality management [9].

DQ Issues

Data quality issues are the problem that occurs to data when implanting ERP system. There are a number of issues involving data quality to be solved which I will discuss briefly in this chapter.

A. Lack of Research

Lack of knowledge and research about data quality management in ERP system, understanding different methods according to quality management is important to improve data quality in an ERP system. This is a well known issue as organizations do not have the required knowledge to ensure security and integrity when implementing an ERP system such as SAP for example.

B. Data Integrity

Process of transferring data or information in ERP systems encounters issues that highly impacts data quality such as losing or damaging data packets is a common problem that occurs in the sending/receiving process of data especially in wireless based data transfer systems.

One of the proposed solutions to avoid losing data packets or reduce the chance of having damaged data is to apply high performance packet switching/transferring architecture to ensure security and integrity of data, however that can be quite expensive to implement in ERP systems, but There are other alternative solutions at less cost such as encrypting the data packets before sending and decrypt it once it's received however, encrypting/decrypting process affects the availability of the data as encrypting/decrypting process takes quite a while to be done.

C. Data Security

Data security issues in general involve a lot of arguments and discussions in a networking point of view, however in ERP system we tend to look at something a bit different and less complex. In ERP data security is defined as securing the process of moving an enterprise information and data from a central database to fully integrated systems which an organization will handle most of its communication and data issues and that will be an ERP system.

D. Data Accessibility

Lack of information data base assets, low level accessibility, security authentication, understand ability, data amounts and required time to access these data has lead to barring data and make it hard to access it and that is also an issue that has not be resolved yet.

CRITICAL SUCCESS FACTORS IMPACTING ON DATA QUALITY IN IMPLEMENTING ERP SYSTEM

Certain factors exist to control DQ in the implementation process of an ERP. Enterprises should consider focusing on these critical success factors depending on the framework, which involves developing, quality management support,

This paper investigates data quality problems in terms of ERP implementations. This study has chosen SAP as ERP system for testing and investigating issues. Also this study has chosen a high level of collecting data and findings analysis. A research of a case study has studied the current experience in its reality context [13] and it has been used when the theory and research were at the starting stages [6]. There isn't that much research done on data quality problems in the context of ERP, therefore we need to know if data quality issue has an impact on organization's decision making when it comes to implementing an ERP system, in addition to defining the critical success factors for ensuring quality of data during ERP implementations. Thus, this case study seemed to be suitable. ERP implementation at different organisation and the system's owner's and users dealing with the major changes of ERP were analysed in this case study. Four types of people with an organization involved in ERP

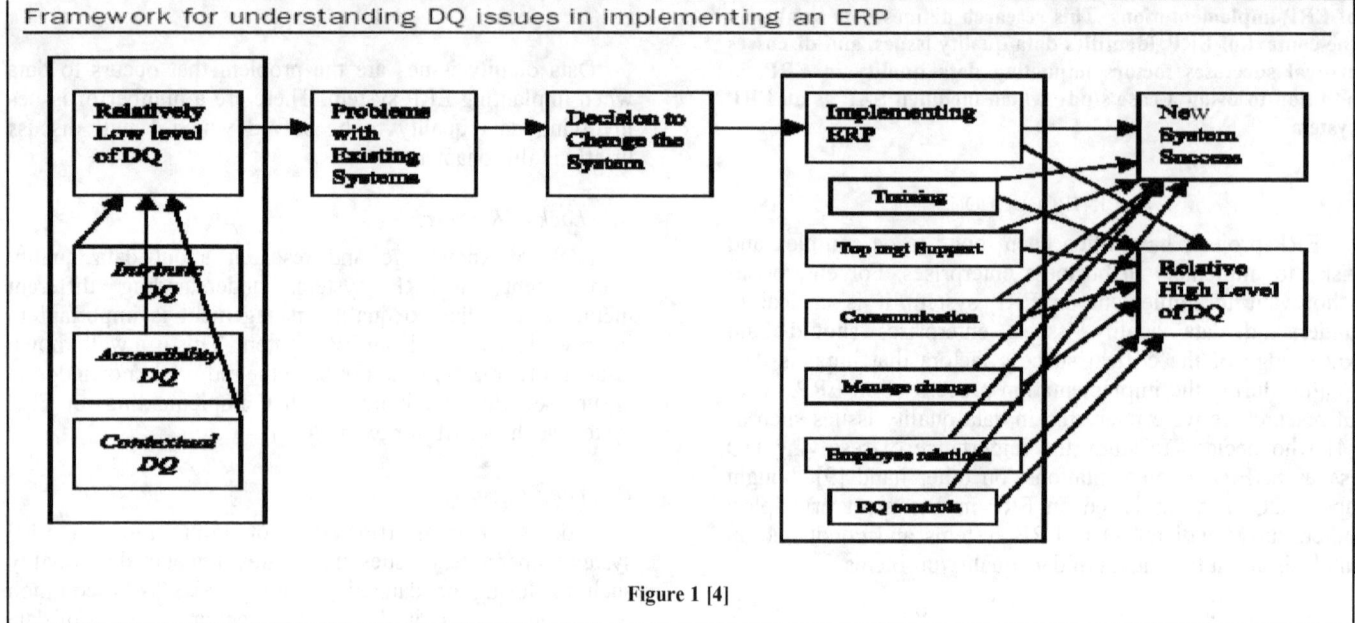

Figure 1 [4]

managing staff changes activities, and data quality. Obtaining information about critical success factors will lead to increasing the level of data quality management, which will be the primary factor to ensure successful ERP implementations. Also gathering information about critical success factors specifications is essential to allow enterprises to gain a better understanding of data quality leading to better control over data quality during ERP implementation process,.

A FRAMEWORK FOR OBTAING KNOWLEGE ABOUT DQ ISSUES IN IMPLEMENTING ERP

Fig. 1 above explains the framework by combining DQ quality issues pattern concepts along with the critical factors concepts in DQ management [9].

have been identified as the following:

1. Data Collectors: people responsible for producing or gathering data in ERP system

2. Data Developers: people involved in designing, developing and operating the ERP system

3. Data Users: people who use the ERP data in their work environment, employees, consumers...etc

4. Data Managers: people who are responsible for managing ERP data and quality management in ERP systems [7].

Collection of data of this case study included interviews with different people involved in ERP implementations, these interviews included data users, data collectors and data developers, however no interviews were made with data managers and the reason behind that was that the two companies that were used in this case study did not have any

What organisations have done in relation to the critical success factors while implementing ERP (SAP)	Company A	Company B
Training	Diverse range of courses related to SAP	Will have large scaled training
Top management support (who made the decision?)	Parent company	The heads of the organisation and the Board
Communications (members of the project team)	Business people and IT people (project team didn't provide adequate documentation of the ERP system for users to follow)	Business people (2/3) IT people (1/3) (more business than IT, because business people would know the requirements of the ERP system)
Manage change	Few months parallel run	A couple of months parallel run, and then move to SAP
Employees relations (how to persuade people to move to an ERP system)	No actions (employee turnover may cause DQ problems)	Don't bother arguing, just say: "it's been decided"
DQ controls (who makes sure of DQ before changing systems?)	Business people: checking DQ in the old system, and implementing DQ controls during ERP implementation	Business people: will have much more checking and reporting during the systems changing process

Table 2 Organisations respond in relation to critical success [4].

data managers for their ERP projects. Data gathering for this case study also provided related documents to the project, such as employee's positions descriptions, organizations policy, organisational structure charts, employee's training information and other irrelevant documents about these companies, such as financial records and annual reports, and the reason behind these information was to investigate how the company is performing during the implementation of an ERP and how what the impact of DQ issues during the ERP project.

FINDINGS

The major people involved in ERP project were interviewed and asked about what they think about the impact of data quality issues in the implementation process of an ERP system. More information was obtained from other sources such as reports, external and internal documents. Finally the conclusion of these findings were summarised in Table 1 and Table 2 above. Table 1 shows the difference before and after applying ERP (SAP) system. And Table 2 shows what these companies have done in the relation to the critical success factors identified earlier in the study's framework [4].

CONCLUSION

Data quality is a major issue in the ERP implementation projects. This paper examined the implementation of an ERP system and used SAP as an example, in addition to proposing a framework for obtaining knowledge about data quality issues that occur during the transfer of data from data bases to an ERP system. A number of issues has been defined and should be studied and considered by an organization when implementing ERP. Critical success factors for data quality during the ERP implementation process were proposed. The case study used in this research

provided information about DQ issues that will lead to better understanding of these issues as well as giving effective information gained from actual ERP projects. The paper also provided a framework for understanding these different issues to help resolve them and ensure fully integrated and secured data.

REFERENCES

[1] Ballou, D.P. and Pazer, H. L. (1982), ``The impact of inspector fallibility one the inspection policy serial production system'', Management Science, Vol. 28 No.4, pp. 387-99.

[2] Ballou, D.P. and Pazer, H.L. (1985), ``Modelling data and process quality in multi-input, multi-output information systems'', Management Science, Vol. 31 No. 2, pp. 150-62.

[3] Xiaosong, Z, 2010. INTRODUCTION. *The Application Study of ERP Data Quality Assessment and Improvement Methodology*, China: Tianjin University.

[4] Hongjiang, X,2001, DQ issues. *Data quality issues in implementing an ERP*: Australia University of Southern Queensland.

[5] Wand, Y. and Wang, R.Y. (1996), ``Anchoring data quality dimensions in ontological.

[6] Benbasat, I., Goldstein, D.K. and Mead, M. (1987), ``The case study research strategy in studies of information systems'', MIS Quarterly, Vol. 11, pp. 369-86.

[7] Strong, D.M., Lee, Y.W. and Wang, R.Y. (1997), ``Data quality in context'', *Communications of the ACM*, Vol. 40 No. 5, pp. 103-10.

[8] SAP AG Corporate Overview (2000), January. Available at: http:\\www.sap.com\company\index.html.

[9] Saraph, J.V., Benson, P.G. and Schroeder, R.G.

[10] (1989), ``An instrument for measuring the critical factors of quality management'', *Decision Sciences*, Vol. 20 No. 4, pp. 810-29.

[11] Huang, H.-T., Lee, Y.W. and Wang, R.Y. (1999), *Quality Information and Knowledge*, Prentice Hall PTR.

[12] Segev, A. (1996), ``On information quality and the WWW impact a position paper'', *Conference of Information Quality*, 15-26 October.

[13] Yin, P.K. (1994), *Case Study Research: Design and Methods*, 2nd ed., Sage.

Strategies for preventing resistance to change when implementing cloud ERP systems

Aaron Armstrong

School of Computing and Mathematics

University of Derby, United Kingdom.

100067017@unimail.derby.ac.uk

Abstract— It is becoming increasingly popular for ERP systems to be moved to the cloud. Despite this, implementing ERP systems suffers from an unusually high failure rate. A key factor in many of these failures is poor change management leading to resistance against the new system. This paper looks at change management, resistance to change and strategies to prevent resistance from occurring.

Keywords; strategies; resistance; change; management; ERP; cloud.

CHANGE MANAGEMENT

One of the main issues to be dealt with during the implementation of an ERP system is change management – how to help the employees of an enterprise transition from using legacy systems to the new system smoothly. Yet it is often overlooked and neglected, leading to the implementation failing. Table 1 contains a survey of 48 Australian companies and what they felt the barriers were to realising the full benefits of ERP [1]. Each barrier was categorised according to the Deloitte Consulting study [2] into "people", "process" or "technology".

This shows why change management is important. In short, people don't always like change. This often boils down to several factors related to a lack of knowledge of the benefits an ERP system can bring. For example, an employee might not understand why a new system is being introduced when they feel they get by ok with the current system, or they may feel the new technology may eventually take over their jobs. Perhaps they feel that they aren't skilled enough to learn how to use a new system. It may just be that staff weren't told why the new system was being introduced, leading to them not really caring due to a lack of knowledge.

All of this leads to resistance - users actively being against the implementation of the new system, often dooming it to failure. Statistics suggest the failure rate of ERP implementations lies between 60-90% [3], a staggering figure. However, it should be pointed out that poor change management is often not the sole reason for failure. Implementing an ERP system is expensive and complicated therefore it requires sufficient planning all around to be a success.

TABLE I.   BARRIERS [1]

Current Barrier	Mean	Deloitte Category
Lack of Discipline	4.4	P
Lack of Change Management	4.3	P
Inadequate Training	4.2	P
Poor Reporting Procedures	4.2	T
Inadequate Process Engineering	3.9	PR
Misplaced Benefit Ownership	3.8	P
Inadequate Internal Staff	3.3	P
Poor Prioritisation of Resources	3.0	T
Poor Software Functionality	2.9	T
Inadequate Ongoing Support	2.7	T
Poor Business Performance	2.4	PR
Under Performed Project Team	2.3	P
Poor Application Management	2.2	T
Upgrades Performed poorly	1.6	T

Wenrich [4] assesses a 10 year period of change management to look at what should and shouldn't be done when implementing a new ERP system. She highlights the important aspects of good change management. The two key areas she identifies to prevent resistance occurring are extensive training for the new system, and full commitment from management to explain the goals of the new system to everyone. Furthermore, she warns against the dangers of underestimating just how much training could be required. Interestingly, a small point made is that special attention should be given to help the users recover from incorrect data entry, thus making the assumption that users are more likely to make input errors while learning a new system.

THE CLOUD

The cloud is an emerging technology in the field of computing, making use of the vast server space available over the internet to provide services. This means that rather than having to own and maintain all the necessary resources for a system, an enterprise can just use the system when it needs it. This removes the high start-up costs of needing to buy/upgrade equipment and the time and responsibility of looking after the system and the machines it runs on. Instead, a running cost is paid to the service provider for the duration that access to the system is required. NIST defines three different server models for cloud providers to provide services: Software as a Service (SaaS), Platform as a Service (PaaS) and Infrastructure as a Service (IaaS). In relation to using a cloud based ERP system, SaaS is the relevant service. SaaS allows an application to be hosted on the cloud and accessible through a medium such as a web browser or desktop application. This can simplify matters greatly for a company. For example, rather than manually having to enter payroll details every month, the hours worked per employee can be sent to the cloud ERP system, which handles everything on its own.

This potentially backs up the aforementioned reason for resistance that employees fear for their jobs. If a new cloud ERP system is capable of doing more of the work, it is only natural to worry that it could make you obsolete in the future.

Although there are concerns about how suited to mission critical systems such as ERP a cloud solution is, they are becoming increasingly popular. This is because cloud services tend to be subscription based, rather than a large initial cost, something that can be extremely tempting for an enterprise to avoid. Also, as was alluded to either, ERP systems can be complicated to deploy and maintain. Moving to the cloud shifts the responsibility for this task from the enterprise to the cloud provider.

A common misconception when it comes to moving the cloud is that it removes the need for change management, as processes are being taken away, simplifying the business. This is not true at all. As with any kind of outsourcing, the people within the business need to given help to adapt to the changes it brings. For example, one of the reasons for resistance given earlier was that of fear of losing their jobs – it is reasonable that an IT support staff member may feel their job is threatened by moving processes away to the cloud if they don't understand why it will help their job rather than take it away.

Implementing a new ERP system on the cloud isn't less traumatic than doing it in house. It is such a large change to an enterprise's ethos, working practices and habits that you could argue it is a complete upheaval. On the other hand, it could be said that the average user won't really know the difference between using a program installed on a local server, or hosted on a cloud. Therefore, maybe the change is no different to many people from installing new software locally.

STRATEGIES

Four strategies for change management are suggested in [5]: Empirical-Rational, Normative-Reeducative, Power-Coercive and Environmental-Adaptive. Although the strategies aren't designed with ERP systems (or even computing in general) in mind, they can still be applied as it is about the people, not the technology.

Empirical-Rational assumes that people are rational and will follow what is best for them. Thus, it promotes change by offering incentives to make the upsides of the change outweigh the downsides. It can work either way however, an incentive may just be enough to make an employee give a new system a chance, which could make all the difference. However, the more cynical employee may see it as an attempt to pull the wool over their eyes, and could actually increase resistance.

Normative-Reeducative focuses on the social and cultural aspects of an enterprise. It comments that most people want to fit in with everyone else. As such, if the enterprise can make the ERP system seem like a good step to most people, the rest will follow willingly. Of course, it isn't possible to make people change their minds overnight so if this strategy was adopted, it would need to done over a long stretch of time, making more and more people view the new system as a good thing. This could potentially be effective in this scenario, as moving to the cloud is such a major cultural change that focusing on the culture could be extremely beneficial.

Power-Coercive is the hard line approach. You accept the new system whether you like it or not, facing punishment if you show resistance to it. It is essentially the opposite of the Empirical-Rational approach as you're attempting to force employee into accepting the system rather than encouraging them to like it. Whether this strategy can succeed for or not often depends on the existing culture at the enterprise. If the employee are used to being told what to do and just getting on with it, it may well succeed. However if the culture isn't like that one, this approach will probably increase resistance.

Environmental-Adaptive suggests that people are naturally good at adapting to change, and that the fear of disruption is only a barrier to that. Interestingly, the solution given is to create a new organisation and gradually move people across. This supposedly removes people's fear of disruption as there is nothing you can do about it, meaning they just get on with adapting. However, it is difficult to see how this would work in reality.

Aladwani [6] suggests a detailed proposal for a change management strategy when implementing an ERP system is proposed. It is a solution containing 3 phases – knowledge formulation, strategy implementation and status evaluation.

The knowledge formulation phase is designed to help the management understand the attitudes of their employees about the new ERP system and where those attitudes come from so that the change management can be tailored to suit their specific needs.

To do this, Aladwani believes the key questions that need to be answered are:

- Who is resisting?
- What do they need?
- What are their values and beliefs?
- What are they interested in?

He believes that answering these questions can give a good insight into why they are resisting the new system, and thus how to combat it.

He then discusses what causes resistance to change and highlights the same issues already discussed, further backing up the role that they play in resistance to change.

The strategy implementation phase is the main body of the change management. He suggests various techniques that can be used in combination.

To change attitude, management must "affect cognitive component of users' attitudes". In other words, the management must find a way to change how their employees think about the new system. As negativity towards change is often borne from a lack of knowledge, Aladwani argues that communication is essential for this. That way, employees can understand the benefits of using both ERP systems and the cloud rather than legacy systems on local servers/machines. There have been several examples of ERP implementation failing because the benefits weren't understood well enough, causing the workforce to be disinterested in the system, ultimately leading to its failure.

However, on the other hand, he warns that selling the benefits to the employees could in fact increase resistance later on. This is about expectations management - if its oversold, employees may expect too much from the system, then become disappointed and disillusioned when it doesn't live up to their hyped expectations. Therefore, it is safe to say that balance in crucial. Impress the need for ERP systems and the cloud, but don't make them out to be the next revolution if they aren't.

Another technique that can be used is to explain how the software operates. Not so much the technical details of the programming, but the general picture of what it can do. For example, SaaS on the cloud allows a company to just send the information required to complete a task, rather than having to actually do the task themselves, thus simplifying it. If this is a particularly mundane task being simplified, this will appeal to the employee responsible for it. This also helps reinforce the message that ERP will help their jobs, not impede them or even replace them.

Also, Aladwani looks at social pressure. This is focusing on getting the most popular and vocal employees to support the new system. The idea here is that once they believe in the new system, others will either want to follow suit and give it a chance or feel like they'll have to or get left behind socially.

Finally there's status evaluation. As its title suggests, this phase is for evaluating the success of the change management. This is to enable the management to assess how well it is going, and make changes if it looks like failing. He states that the information should be "timely, accurate and systematic". Also, it means that the information they find can be stored for a later use, for example another system implementation further down the line. Interestingly, this creates a circle as is often seen in implementation itself – do something, evaluate it, improve it, evaluate it and so on.

CONCLUSIONS

It is clear to see that despite the obvious importance of change management when implementing an ERP system, especially when also moving to the cloud, it is still often neglected. That Table 1 has five of the top seven results people related is just staggering. With such a high failure rate, it is imperative that change management starts to be taken more seriously. Moving to the cloud also increases the need for change management. The dramatic change to culture, working practices, the technical shift and general disruption means that extra effort should be made to make the transition as smooth as possible for everyone.

The strategies suggested in [4] offer a lot of potential. Four different ideas for how to handle change management offers much scope for working out what is best for each scenario. The Empirical-Rational strategy in particular has the potential to be successful. The majority of employees will always react well to incentives, as long as they are significant enough to make a difference. While it could be argued against on the grounds of cost, it would be far costlier for the ERP integration to fail. Aladwani's ideas in [5] provide a coherent strategy specifically created with ERP implementation in mind. Although he doesn't cover moving to the cloud (indeed his paper predates the rise of the cloud), the basic ideas he suggests are very solid and applicable to a wide range of issues, including the cloud. In fact, like with new ERP systems, moving to the cloud's main source of resistance is likely to be that lack of knowledge about it. Therefore, the same steps to improve that knowledge should be taken to combat that.

It is clear to see that much research has done into what causes resistance when implementing ERP systems and moving to the cloud. Yet despite this, too many implementations fail. This leads to an alternate conclusion – the problem may not just be the employees resisting change as that is an obstacle that can be overcome. Instead, the main issue may actually be the common underestimation of how important it is to combat that resistance to change.

REFERENCES

[1] P. Hawking, "Benefit Realisation and ERP systems", 2003.

[2] Deloitte, "ERPs second wave", Deloitte Consulting, 1999.

[3] K. Kwahk, J. Lee, "The role of readiness for change in ERP implementation: Theoretical bases and empirical validation", 2008.

[4] K. I. Wenrich, "Lessons Learned During a Decade of ERP Experience: A Case Study", 2007.

[5] F. Nicholls, "Four Change Management Strategies", 2010.

[6] A. M. Aladwani, "Change management strategies for successful ERP implementation", 2001.

Customer Relationship Management for Small and Medium-sized Enterprises

SaaS a best fit

Adam Jackson
Business Computing and Law
University of Derby Derbyshire
100226667@unimail.derby.ac.uk

Abstract – Software as a Service (SaaS) is vast becoming the norm in the business world, offering up low cost ways of managing business processors. With economic times hard more large enterprises are dispensing with their in-house ERP systems removing operational and maintenance costs, and have began to embrace Cloud services. The Cloud claims to offer better access, reduction in costs as well as boost efficiency, all of which make it an attractive prospect for large enterprises looking to streamline business operational procedures and thus reduce cost. With the adoption rate of SaaS in large enterprise and the numerous benefits on offer it is now becoming a feasible option for SMEs (Small Medium Enterprises), opening up opportunities that they once thought where only reserved for much larger businesses.

Keywords: SaaS, ERP, CRM, SME'S, Risk, BOP

Background

A. Software as a service

The buzzword in the Information Technology world at the moment is Cloud computing, Cloud computing is the distribution of computing as a service as opposed to a product. Resources that are distributed across the cloud range from information to software packages. When software is offered over the Cloud it is known as Software as a service. Software as a service known by its abbreviation SaaS is as mentioned a form of digital software distribution.

The software applications on offer in the Cloud vary between vendors. The distributed software applications are not downloaded by users they are however hosted on remote servers owned by the Cloud vendors. To access the server an agreement needs to be arranged with a Cloud vendor. Cloud vendors operate on a subscription bases ranging from a single month subscription onwards. Once an agreement has been entered into the users are given access to their selected services. To access those services the customer only needs to access the vendors website and log in with the credentials provided to them from the registration with the vendor. From there they have access to their new services and can begin working in the Cloud.

Some of the benefits of the cloud as advertised by SaaS vendors:-

- Ease of implementation
- Ease of use
- Pay for what you need
- High Scalability
- High flexibility

A. Why focus on Small Medium sized Enterprises

Small medium size enterprises play a pivotal role in the European economy and represent 99% of all enterprises. Within the enlarged European Union of 25 countries there are somewhere in the region of 23 million SMEs which provide approximately 75 million jobs.

Business process outsourcing is the process of transferring business processors to a third party SaaS vendor. Traditionally things like Customer Relationship Management or CRM were only associated with large enterprises, mainly because they had the infrastructure and money to put them in place. CRM systems were just not viable for SME's be it from a financial or a functional view point, however that was before the onset of SaaS and the Cloud. In-house CRM systems are expensive to install, the same functionality is now available online from the Cloud on a subscription bases. Now a SME can open an account with a SaaS vendor for a month and sample a CRM system and see if it is a fit for their business, without costing them the bank.

Investigation

This report will look at SaaS and BPO for SMEs

A. What SaaS brings to an SME

Businesses invest money into Information Technology continually to improve business functionality and performance, but at the same time they are aware that value needs to be derived from doing so.
SMEs are more concerned with deriving value from their IT investments as they do not have the same amount of capital that large enterprises do.
With SMEs a poor decision relating to IT investments can have a large negative impact on their profitability [1]. In some instances the cost and risk involved with incorporating IT solutions can both exceed the budget and capabilities of the SME. IT costs do not just cover the purchase and installation of hardware and suitable software but may also include implementation costs (staff training), maintenance and upgrade costs and running costs. All these expenses are difficult to initially calculate but do mount up.

SaaS alleviates the issues of implementing a high cost IT system and provides a stable IT platform for SMEs. SaaS can bring a lot to an enterprise, gone are the days where having a CRM system costs thousands of pounds, accruing all of the hardware and software need to run the system as well as other. SaaS vendors like Salesforce.com allow customers to simply log onto their online service and pay to access a online CRM system from an internet browser.

Removing the cost of the hardware and software consumers are purchasing access to the software through the site. Payment methods such as pay for what you use are available and so are monthly payments. SaaS is treated like any of utility such as gas and electric. Offering up flexibility and allowing for a pay for what you use model and for as long as it is needed.

B. The use of a CRM in an SME

Customer relationship management (CRM) refers to any and all interactions between customers and clients. CRM software is designed to process, organize and synchronize a multitude of processes across a business. These processes can be anything from sales, marketing, customer services and technical support.

As mentioned earlier in the report traditionally SME's haven't had much in the way of CRM systems do to the cost of them. Now SaaS vendors can offer CRM and other ERP systems at a fraction of the cost of in-house solutions.

Know your customer systems also known as KYC are systems that are used to confirm the identity and creditability of potential customer, this is important when a SME moves into a new market. These are also available on the Cloud from SaaS Vendors.

Giving a SME access to an online CRM opens up the availability of the information to the SME. With Smart technology such as Phones and Tablets having inbuilt web browsers the data stored on the Cloud CRM can now be accessed anywhere at any time. This gives the SME unprecedented access to their information and allows decisions to be made away from the office. Now longer does a company have to wait for the manager to arrive before a sale can go through, now that data can be accessed remotely and a decision made.
One of the pioneering providers in the SaaS space is Salesforce.com offering its CRM application as a service. Other examples of SaaS vendors are Google's web based office applications offering word processing, spreadsheets etc, Microsoft online CRM, or Adobe Photoshop and Adobe Premier on the web.

C. SaaS a key enabler to SME growth

In the past business growth relied on profit and the reinvestment of that profit into the business allowing for growth and development. Within large firms that made sense and was viable because of high turnover and the infrastructure to do so. SMEs though don't have that kind of opportunity the money they made was used to reinvest in themselves but growth was something that took years. Trying a new things was a risky endeavor be it a potential new product or a new IT system. SMEs unlike large enterprises just could not afford the risk of branching out as the outcome of such an endeavor could be potential devastating to the SMEs. With the onset of Cloud that expansion can be achieved at a reduce cost. With SaaS vendors offering solutions such as KYC allowing a business to check out potential new clients or partnerships at low cost growth for SMEs is now more affordable.
The internet and ecommerce allowing a business that was once regional to become multinational overnight at the click of a button.

The cloud enables that adaptability and scalability to happen overnight no more do you need to investment in a product that might not have the market penetration that you want. Now something can be considered from the CRM data and developed and disrupted. Instead of a product reaching within the same country as the business, the internet and the cloud allows a company to reach a wider market, further increasing reach and profit.

The internet is easy to use and with millions of people accessing the internet each day there are very few SMEs that don't have a web presence. [3] Being on the internet and utilizing it is one of the biggest catalysts for growth coupling that with SaaS and BOP.

In-house considerations
Requires CRM to be tight integrate into companies existing business processors
Expensive to implement
Maintenance cost is high
Expensive upgrades
Requires specialized data structures
Already invested in IT infrastructure both support and resource systems

Cloud considerations
Get up and running quickly
Implementing your first CRM solution wanting to determine what will work best before committing to an on premise solution
Low cost implementation
Maintenance cost taken care of by vendor
Upgrades are handled by vendor at no cost to client
Requires little customization

Conclusion

Cloud computing is still evolving and will continue to evolve for years to come. Much like the internet did from its initial conception to what we have today. As it stands the cloud is becoming more viable for SMEs and offers a wealth of benefits and with advances in the Cloud space and IT the Cloud will be even more efficient and beneficial in the future.

One of the major advantages of a Cloud based CRM solutions are the scalability that they offer a business. This scalability allows a business to start with a small amount of storage space and then increase that storage space as necessary when the business expands. Additionally with a Hosted CRM the need for costly upgrades is removed unlike that off an in-house CRM. Without the frequent upgrades the businesses operational costs go down. Hosted services also provide secure, reliable storage that removes the need to backup onsite to multiple hard drives.

The cost to benefit is another compelling reason that SME's are adopting the SaaS approach to business management and business streamlining. No longer do manager of SME have to tip toe around when it comes to IT investments, now they can purchase access to a SaaS vendors services and test out a new system at minimal cost risk free without being locked into a contract which is supplying them with resource they don't need and a service that doesn't work for them. SMEs now can log onto the Cloud and sample some of the services that large enterprise have been enjoying for years. Sampling without huge upfront costs and carrying very little risks. With the streamlining that Cloud brings some of the weight of being an SME manager is removed.

The Estimated service market share of BPO represents around 25% of all services markets in 2009, this has surely risen since then. [4]

REFERENCES

[1] J. Ballantine, M. Levy, P. Powell, Firm size and the evaluation of information systems: issues and evidence, in: Proceedings of the European Conference on Information Systems, Lisbon, Portugal, 2–4 July, 1996, pp. 797–809.[3] J. Ballantine, R. Galliers, S. Stray, Inform

[2] Service Specification in Cloud Environments Based on Extensions to Open Standards

[3] B. S. a. S. S. Hamid R Motahari-Nezhad, "Outsourcing Business to Cloud Computing: Opportunities and Challenges," p. 18, 2009.

[4] C. Anderson, et al. Worldwide and US Business Process Outsourcing 2007-2011 Forecast: Market Oppurtunities by Horizontal Business Process, IDC Market Analysis 208290, Sept. 2007.

How can cloud computing help develop, maintain, and ensure the success of an Information System (IS) in Small to Medium Businesses (SMB)

Alex Nazaruk
School of Computing
University of Derby
Derby, United Kingdom
alex@penoval.co.uk

Abstract—**A definition of Information Systems is presented, along with a presentation of research into the factors that contribute to the success or failure of an Information System. Cloud Computing is introduced, the benefits of which are explored in moderate detail. Finally a case is assembled with a view to promote the use of cloud computing in an attempt to ensure the success of an Information System for Small to Medium sized businesses.**

Information System; Cloud Computing; Small to Medium Sized Businesses; Systems Success and Failure; Software as a Service, Platform as a Service; Infrastructure as a Service;

INTRODUCTION

When approaching the issues of Small to Medium sized businesses and how they can ensure the successful implementation of an Information System, there are many aspects to be considered. It must be looked at how and why Information Systems might fail for these enterprises, taking into account major factors that contribute to these. A possible solution and methodology must be sourced and introduced along with a justification and rationale as to why the solution would be beneficial in these circumstances.

WHAT IS AN INFORMATION SYSTEM (IS)?

Information Systems (IS) are widely used in business to assist, improve, restructure or innovate one or multiple workflows. Yeo defines that IS consists of a combination of hardware, communication technologies and software designed to handle the flow of information from these workflows.[1] Some examples of the types of industries that use IS are banking, insurance and travel. Yeo speaks of the implementation of an IS requiring designing, delivery and actual use of the system before it can be deemed completed.[1]

WHAT FACTORS CONTRIBUTE TO THE SUCCESS OR FAILURE OF AN IS?

When determining whether implementation of an IS has succeeded of failed we first need to determine a measure of success. It has been said that we can use these three labels to denote the extent of which an IS has succeeded or failed;[2]

- Total Failure
  A system may have been planned, researched and possibly even built but never implemented or immediately abandoned during implementation.

- Partial Failure
  The system may have been implanted but primary goals may have never been reached or there may have been a number of undesired results that reduce the effectiveness of the system.

- Success
  The system has been implemented, meeting all primary goals without experiencing any undesired results that hinder the operation of the system.

However, further research uncovers several other factors which should also be considered when attempting to produce a successful IS. These are explored below.

E. Development time

Development time is expensive The more overrun development of a system becomes, an increase is seen in the overall cost of implementing an IS. This could seriously affect the viability of implementing such a system for Small to Medium sized business enterprises which may not have the funds or time available to dedicate to the implementation.

F. Development and running costs

IS require initial hardware & development investment to first implement the system, along with continuing financial outgoings to maintain operability of the systems. Often a business will cater for the operability of a system at peak times, requiring more hardware to serve its user base than is required at the majority of times. This leads to higher average running costs than would typically be required were it not for these usage spikes that may only appear a few times in a year.

G. Interaction Failure

If a system or the underlying hardware becomes overwhelmed and is unable to function, it's users will no longer be able to gain access and use the system for its desired purpose, or maybe gain access only to a lesser extent, leaving businesses with a system that fails to provide the service it was intended to.[1] Also falling under the category of interaction failure comes poor software design that fails to achieve a usability level of which the average user can master.

WHAT IS CLOUD COMPUTING?

Cloud computing utilizes the power of large server farms to provide scalable solutions for individuals and businesses. There is some evidence to prove that, using cloud computing, initial investment costs and longer-term running costs can be reduced. The evidence for these is presented below.

H. Hardware benefits

An organization that decides to use Cloud Computing to implement an IS will have certain advantages when it comes to the required amount of, and cost of, the hardware that they require.[3]

As hardware in the cloud is owned by, and maintained by the organization providing the Cloud Computing service, initial outgoings on hardware are reduced, since the business that is using the Cloud Computing service no longer has the obligation to source and install their own hardware to operate their IS needs.

Furthermore, ongoing running costs can be reduced by using an on-demand approach to scale up or down the amount of hardware that they require to operate their systems, to the level of traffic and load that the system is currently experiencing.

To summarize, cloud computing can reduce infrastructure costs. A knock-on effect to this is that energy costs for running the hardware will not be incurred, since the hardware no longer has to be installed and operated by the business that uses it.

I. Software benefits

As hardware will not have to be installed and configured by the business that wishes to use it, and a number of pre-configurations are readily available on the cloud, companies can begin their software development immediately without the need to wait for the hardware to become installed and available. This can lead to a faster time to market for the IS and in turn begin to generate profit and/or begin reducing operating costs in a shorter timeframe.

Also due to the availability of a mass amount of hardware if required, the software can be scaled to take advantage of whatever hardware it requires at a given time without the need to restructure the backend in a complex manner. Additional server can simply be cloned an linked in a short amount of time to expand the operating abilities of the IS.

J. Core technological models of cloud computing

Cloud Computing consists of several operating layers of the architecture. These are commonly known as Software as a Service, Platform as a Service, and Infrastructure as a service.[3]

1) Software as a Service (SaaS)

In Software as a Service, an application actually runs on the cloud, thus negating the need to have installed it on any clients computers. This provides an obvious advantage in terms of Accessibility and Availability, allowing the software to be accessed from a variety of locations and across a variety of different platforms. Examples of these are applications such as Gmail, Google Apps, Facebook or Twitter.

2) Platform as a Service (PaaS)

A Platform as a Service utilizes the hardware available on the cloud to allow operation of a software application directly without the need and cost of buying the underlying software and hardware.

3) Infrastructure as a Service (IaaS)

Infrastructure as a service differs slightly from the aforementioned models in that it offers only storage and computational power as a service without the need and associated cost of purchasing your own server equipment or setting up your own datacenter. Examples of IaaS could be the Amazon S3 storage service and the Amazon EC2 computing platform.

USING CLOUD COMPUTING TO ENSURE THE SUCCESS OF AN IS IN SMB'S

When looking at the factors of success of an IS and the potential benefits of cloud computing that have already been mentioned a case can be built for the use of Cloud Computing to ensure success of an IS in small to medium sized businesses.

Firstly, when looking at the development time of an IS, we can negate the need to set up a backend hardware infrastructure and immediately begin development and rapid deployment of the IS using the hardware and platforms or software made available to us by the cloud.

Secondly, when looking at the initial investment required to provide a platform for our IS, we can remove the need for initial hardware investment, which in turn reduces the need for investment in physical space or new premises in which to house this equipment.

Furthermore, running and maintenance costs could also be lowered through the use of the cloud, due to the fact that it is the organization who hosts the Cloud services that endures the costs of maintaining and running the equipment, which includes savings on servicing, energy costs and the costs of employees to perform these actions.

In 2010, Ali-Khajeh-Hosseini et al. performed a case study into the migration of an enterprise IT system to IaaS. They noted that using cloud computing the organization in question would have achieved savings of up to 37% on their system infrastructure costs over a five year period [Table 1]. They also noted that a figure of up to 21% of support calls could have been reduced for the same system. [4]

In addition, S. Marston et al. presented an argument that for Small to Medium sized businesses, Cloud Computing is a cost effective way to deploy IT solutions. [3]

TABLE II.   COMPARISON OF COSTS BETWEEN HOSTING A SYSTEM ON THE CLOUD OR SELF-HOSTING.

Period	Cloud Cost	Original Cost
1 Month	£390	£620
1 Year	£4,680	£7,440
5 Years	£23,400	£37,200

II. CONCLUSIONS

There are many factors that affect the viability of Information Systems, Including Implementation and Running costs, usability of the system, abandonment of the system and failure to meet all of the required goals when implementing the system.

The research presented here shows that by migrating or implementing a system using Cloud Computing, A number of benefits can be achieved that help with the elimination of the possible failure of the system.

Empirical evidence has been gathered that shows in no uncertain terms the savings that could be achieved using cloud computing.

REFERENCES

[7]   K.T. Yeo, "Critical failure factors in information system projects", International Journal of Project Management, vol. 20, pp.241–246, 2002.

[8]   Richard Heeks, "Information Systems and Developing Countries: Failure, Success, and Local Improvisations", The Information Society, vol. 18, pp.101–112, 2002.

[9]   Sean Marston, Zhi Li, Subhajyoti Bandyopadhyay, Juheng Zhang, Anand Ghalsasi, "Cloud computing — The business perspective", Decision Support Systems, vol. 51, pp.176–189, 2011

[10] Ali Khajeh-Hosseini, David Greenwood, Ian Sommerville, "Cloud Migration: A Case Study of Migrating an Enterprise IT System to IaaS", Cloud Computing (CLOUD) (2010) IEEE 3rd International Conference 450-457.

Approaches to managing security concerns in cloud ERP

Aneil Chall

University of Derby
Information Technology Year 3
Derby, UK

ABSTRACT

This paper looks into the security problems that have occurred in cloud ERP and some ways of managing those problems to the best standard. I will identify three major security problems currently and give examples of failures and suggest approaches that might overcome those issues.

INTRODUCTION

The positive advantages of cloud computing are well-known and can be summarised as follows:

•   Reduced costs: Cloud technology is paid for on the basis of what you need, which this can save organisations money in the short term.

•   Increased Storage: Much greater amounts of data can be stored by an organisation than on private computer systems

•   Highly automated: A company's IT staff don't need to keep software up to date as maintenance is the job of the service provider on the cloud.

•   More mobility: Employees are able   access information wherever they are, instead of being tied to company computers

However, this is developing, complicated technology so there are there are also downsides to considering cloud computing, largely to do with the security and privacy of data and the loss of control over it.

This is an even greater concern when it comes to companies that wish to keep their sensitive information on cloud servers. While most service vendors would ensure that their servers are kept free from viral infection and malware, it Is essential to understand the nature of the cloud . A number of users from around the world are accessing the servers. Ensuring that a client's data is not accessed by any unauthorised users is of great importance. The loss of control is a major reason against using cloud applications and data storage for an organisation's computing.

This paper argues that control should only be passed on with great care being taken and with suitable back-up for applications and data in case things go wrong.   An organisation must do its best to ensure that a cloud provider delivers reliability and liability; data security, privacy and anonymity; and no access and usage restrictions on the service. At the same time, the organisation should assume there will be failure and plan for it.

Some of the failures have happened within the cloud networks of very major companies including Google, Amazon, Salesforce, Skype and Twitter.

Google for example had a global outage of Gmail in September 2009 (GmailBlog, 2009, cited in Gumawi et al, 2011) and then in February 2010 experienced a power failure that affected a quarter of the machines in the data centre. The system that was designed to quickly recover failed as the engineers had failed to plan for this particular case (Google, 2010, cited in Gunawi et al, 2011). Google has experienced cyber-attack and hacking; the source of this was traced to China (Markoff and Barboza, 2010, cited in Bisong and Rahman, 2011).

In December 2001 Skype had some overloads that caused a third of its super nodes to go down. The rest of the super nodes couldn't handle it and so sent traffic back into the network and that led to nearly total outage (Skype.com, 2010, cited in Gunawi et al, 2011) and since then there have been other Skype outages.

Amazon 2011 engineers attempted to upgrade network capacity and network traffic was shifted to the wrong router.

The Sony PlayStation 3 Network was hacked in April 2011 with the exposure and theft of 77 million customers' personal information, and this resulted in the network being down for 24 days. Sony didn't encrypt the user's data and the hacker was able to view sensitive profile data The information that was stolen may have included the customer's credit card details and expiration date (Li, 2011).

This article believes that are 3 main factors that should be considered:

- The human factor

- The security of data-at-rest

- The need for service and data back-up

The human factor is the most common weakness in cloud computing. People may follow weak password discipline, leave cloud applications running on open devices, use devices that already carry malware or hacking tools, make poor decisions about the location or encryption of data files or a service level agreement with a cloud provider. Because the cloud system is so complex, it only needs one weak link in a public cloud to possibly put the rest of the cloud users at risk (Kaufman, 2009, cited in Subashini and Kavita, 2011). They consider that in a cloud the risk is 'overwhelmingly high' (p 9). This is because of 'cloud vulnerability and the asset value of the resources and the nature of them residing together' (p 9).

In order to keep data at rest from being accessed, stolen, or altered by unauthorised people, security measures such as data encryption and hierarchical password protection are commonly used with land-based systems. There is no standard policy on encryption offered by cloud providers, and there are many more possible breaches. A recent report (Ponemon Institute, 2011, cited in Li, 2011) shows that cloud providers don't see security as their top priority. About 74% of US and European cloud providers said their services did not strongly protect customers' sensitive data; about 62% of the providers were not confident that their cloud services are highly secure; about 69% of them do not think they have the responsibility for data security and most of them do not have dedicated security personnel. Subashini and Kavita (2011) look at the sources of data breaches and conclude that external criminals offer the greatest threat but may have the smallest impact overall, partners offer less threat but make greater impact, and insider breaches that will be smallest in number will make the greatest impact. Security policy control agreements

become even more important in cloud computing. Evidence reviewed by Khorshed et al (2012) suggests that although security issues stop more organisations from signing up, there are some who don't have a clear understanding of the security problems and even when they ask cloud providers the right questions they sometimes don't get them answered properly and providers do not work with enough transparency. Companies still use price as the main deciding factor when signing up.

Data and service recovery is a huge factor for any company, and they must have back-up plans available. If they are relying on a single cloud provider, a company will be in serious trouble if they can't access data or applications that they need if these are all delivered by cloud. Cloud providers might have reliability problems, or even go out of business. There can be data ownership or right to access issues, due to the location of the servers it is held in or in trying to move data to another provider. Some experts suggest that data could be 'held captive by providers' (Schneier and Ranum, 2009, cited in Khorshed et al, 2010).

For example, an online storage service called The Linkup shut down in August 2008 after losing access to about 45% of customer data (Brodkin, 2008, cited in Ambrust et al, 2010). The Linkup had relied on another online storage service Nirvanix to store customer data, and the responsibility for the data loss was therefore disputed. Eventually The Linkup's 20,000 users were told the service was no longer available.

The problems mentioned in this paper may be enough on their own to stop more companies investing in cloud computing until there are security and service standards in agreed and in use across all cloud providers, and customers have a better understanding of the issues involved. But even the helpful guidance for customers given in large reports (eg ENISA, 2009) gets out of date quickly as researchers get a greater understanding of the large number of ways that the cloud is vulnerable (eg Korshed at al, 2012).

How should a company make sure that their use of the cloud is as secure as possible? There is an increasing amount of helpful advice available (eg Li, 2011; Khorshed et al, 2012) which is of a specialist nature. This makes it very important that a company does not lose IT staff when they move services to cloud, instead they should let them work on the new challenges that the cloud brings to a company.

Looking first at responses to the human challenge, a company must educate and supervise all staff that have access, and a carefully prepared IT security policy must be part of this that staff sign and have reviews about. Permissions or access rights must be set carefully and reviewed often. Passwords must be set to give a high level of security, or access might be given by using a 'card reader' with a PIN required to generate unique, one-time eight-digit codes, as used to gain access to online bank accounts. A proper enforceable password policy will be signed by staff as part of the security document. The system must make a real-time record of logins, identifying staff identity, areas accessed and when.

There also must be guarantees from cloud providers about their policies. Some authors (eg Khorshed et al, 2012) discuss ways that cloud providers should deal with 'malicious insiders' and that should be known to their clients. They conclude their discussion by saying 'Unfortunately in the foreseeable future, it is likely to continue to be a natural tendency of a cloud provider to hide its company policy regarding hiring of employees and put in place insufficient measures to monitor them because of economic reasons' (p839).

The only certain way to protect sensitive data in a cloud environment is not to put it there at all. That seems to be the advice given by some commentators. Customers need to insist on transparency about exactly how data will be encrypted and kept separate from that of other users and get guarantees through service-level agreements. They could retain sensitive data in a completely separate private cloud (evidence presented in Subashini and Kavitha, 2011). Li (2011) points out exactly how the Sony PS3 problem that exposed so much private information should have been prevented.

Khorshed et al (2011) give detailed procedures that cloud providers and customers could use to predict and detect attacks.

With regard to area 3, data loss, companies should always know that providers have a service and data back-up plan in store so if something major was to occur they would be able to act fast and prevent a major service outage or data loss from occurring. Gunawi et al (2011) consider a range of major incidents that involved failures that started automatic recovery systems that did not work as expected and therefor an outrage took place. This should a top priority for any

cloud provider and a client should know about their procedures in detail before trusting them with their data. A cloud system needs to ensure that the recovery strategies work to the best possible standard. Gunami et al (2011) describe large-scale failure tests that cloud providers can run that will help develop more reliable systems, a bit like fire drills.

Li (2011) considers that data must be made as secure as possible by design, and believes that there should be agreed standards in cloud computing. He says that it is very important for customers to know the data management policy at the cloud vendor site. All cloud providers should follow strict policy, likely to include data being replicated to its mirror at a different location when it reaches storage in order to protect the data in the case of problems on one location. The storage server should use up-to-date anti-virus software, as well as a full back-up and disaster recovery strategy. The provider should be compliant with all relevant laws and best practice on data protection. The location of off-site data bunkers should be in highly secure areas with 24/7 security. Li gives an example 'the underground of mountains' (p227).

As cloud providers might not have transparent policies or might not do what they say, the answer could be for a customer to also have some independent back-up of data, perhaps from another cloud provider.

CONCLUSIONS

From researching and understanding the security concerns involved in cloud computing it seems clear that customers need to take responsibility to manage their security concerns in cloud based ERP. Before a user gives his personal data over to the cloud they need to be aware of how the cloud provider will deal with their data, including data segregation and storage, including pack-up. They will need to know about the employment and disciplinary policy of the provider, and be informed about what incidents had previously happened. They will need to get a detailed, service level agreement form the supplier. Their own practices must be as strong as possible. Companies might decide that they will not put their most sensitive data on the cloud network at all.

REFERENCES

Armbrust, M., Fox, A., Griffith, R., Joseph, A.D., Katz, R.,

Konwinski, A., Lee, G., Patterson, D., Rabkin, A, Stoica, I., and Zaharia, M. (2009) Above the Clouds: A Berkeley View of Cloud Computing UC Berkeley Reliable Adaptive Distributed Systems Laboratory.

Bisong, A. and Rahman, S.M. (2011) An overview of the security concerns in enterprise cloud computing. International Journal of Network Security and Its Applications (IJNSA) Vol.3, No.1, January 2011.

Brodkin, J. Loss of customer data spurs closure of online storage service 'The Linkup'. Network World (August 2008).

Butler, B (2012) Amazon outage one year later: Are we safer? Accessed online at http://www.pcadvisor.co.uk/news/security/3354385/amazon -outage-one-year-later-are-we-safer/#ixzz1u9CZB4KJ

Chen, Y., Paxson, V. and Katz, R.H. (2010) What's New About Cloud Computing Security? CS Division, EECS Dept. UC Berkeley

ENISA (2009) Cloud Computing: Benefits, risks and recommendations for information security. European Network and Information Security Agency

GmailBlog.(2009) More on today's Gmail issue http://gmailblog.blogspot.com/20009/more-on-todays-gmail-issue.html, September 20099/

Google.(2010) Post-mortem for February 24th, 2010 outage. https://groups.google.com/group/ google-appengine/browse_thread/thread/a7640a2743922dcf, February 2010.

Gunawi, S.H., Do, T.,Hellerstein, M.H., Stoica, I., Borthakur, D. and Robbins, J. (2011). Failure as a Service (FaaS): A Cloud Service for Large-Scale, Online Failure Drills. University of California at Berkeley.

Heiser J and Nicolett M.(2009) Assessing the security risks of cloud computing. Gartner Report.

Jansen, W. and Grance, T. (2011) Guidelines on Security and Privacy in Public Cloud Computing. National Institute of Standards and Tecnology, US Department of Commerce.

Khorshed, Md.T., Ali, S., and Wasimi, S.A. (2012).A survey on gaps, threat remediation challenges and some thought for proactive detection in cloud computing. Future Generation Computer Systems 28 (2012) p.833-851.

Li, X (2011) Cloud Computing: Introduction, Application and Security from Industry Perspectives. IJCSNNS International Journal 0f Computer Science and Network Security, VOL 11 No.5, May 2011

Markoff, J. Barboza, D. (2010, February 18), 2 China Schools Said to Be Tied to OnlineAttacks. Retrieved from http://www.nytimes.com/2010/02/19/technology/19china.html

Mirzael, N (2008) Cloud Computing. Accessed online at http://grids.ucs.indiana.edu/ptliupages/publications/ReportNarimanMirzaeiJan09.pdf

Schneier, B. and Ranum, M. (2009) Face-off: Assessing cloud computing risks. Retrieved from http://searchcloudsecurity.techtarget.com/video/Face-off-Assessing-cloud-computing-risks.

Skype.com. (2010) CIO update: Post-mortem on the Skype outage (December 2010). http://blogs. skype.com/en/2010/12/cio_update.html,December 2010.

Spring, J.(2011) Monitoring cloud computing by layer, part 1: Security and Privacy. IEEE 9 (2) (2011) P.66-68

Subashini, S. and Kavith, V. (2011), A survey on security issues in service delivery models of cloud computing. Journal of Network and Computer Applications 34 (2011) p.1-11

Summary of Key Security Concerns in Cloud ERP Systems and what can be Done to Combat Them

Benjamin James Hall
School of Computing
University of Derby
Derby, United Kingdom

Abstract — **Cloud technologies have become more popular in recent years due to a number of key benefits. Amongst these benefits are reduced costs, reduced maintenance and greater access to services. Because of this, there is no wonder why an increasing number of organizations are looking towards this technology to improve the efficiency of their business while cutting costs.**

This article investigates the most important security concerns with regards to cloud computing and ERP cloud computing in particular. It also looks at what actions can be taken in order to combat these threats. With an increased uptake of this type of technology, security issues are becoming more frequent and high profile.

Keywords - ERP; security; cloud computing; security strategies; security threats; physical security

INTRODUCTION

Over the past few years, computing has begun to move away from a centralised model, and more towards the cloud. This move has been fueled by the influx of consumer products such as Laptops, PCs, Smartphones and more recently, tablet computers. The use of applications such as DropBox and Google Docs to store files in the cloud enable consumers to access their files on whichever device they like as long as there is an internet connection available. With many devices now having access to either mobile internet or WiFi, this is becoming increasingly more practical.

There is evidence of this trend with the launch recently of iCloud from Apple[1]. This service allows users of its apple products to store files, music and photos on the iCloud and have the ability to push this content to all other devices.

Traditionally, people have stored all their files and documents locally on hard disk drives or DVDs. Photos, music and documents stored on a computer hard drive are only able to be accessed from that one location. The same is true with mobile devices also, where contacts details have been stored on the phone alone. With the cloud, it enables these resources to be accessed from anywhere and it also acts as a backup service. If a computer's hard drive was to fail, it would not mean that all data is not lost, and it will still be accessible from the cloud. Important files will be saved online and is a useful fallback point in case of disk drive issues. The cloud is especially useful when it comes to migrating data from one phone to another.

This same trend can be seen when looking at businesses, and in particular ERP systems. An ERP system allows a company to co-ordinate its activities and provides greater control and efficiency for the company. Traditionally, these systems were run on large mainframe computer systems on site. These systems were expensive, not very customisable and can require expert knowledge to maintain. ERP providers have begun to offer cloud ERP services which allow for greater customisation, greater scalability and are easier to maintain.

Cloud computing carries many benefits, but also many potential risks in terms of security. A user has much greater control over their data if it is stored locally. How does the user know that the data is secure when they are using cloud services? With their data technically accessible from anywhere, what measures are in place to prevent security breaches? This paper looks at the most common security concerns in relation to cloud ERP services and explains what strategies are in place to prevent any breaches.

CLOUD ERP SYSTEMS

Traditional ERP systems are expensive, not very customisable and can require expert knowledge to maintain. ERP providers have begun to offer cloud ERP services which allow for greater customisation, greater scalability and are easier to maintain. In the near future we will see such systems have a greater uptake with larger companies using them to make great cost savings[2].

Hoffman claims that could ERP systems will eventually win out in the battle against traditional systems due to two main technologies, multi-core and Web2.0. These technologies combined are making the cloud more accessible to more people. The potential ability to control ERP systems from smartphones or tablet computers gives companies a competitive edge over its rivals, in increasing efficiency and reducing costs. Such an idea appears to becoming reality as Intel has revealed that it intends to make $1bn savings using cloud technologies to promote more effective and efficient use of its data.

I. SECURITY

With the increase in popularity in cloud ERP systems, there are security concerns which need to be addressed when moving from traditional in-house systems to those in the cloud. With traditional systems, the client usually has control over what happens on their computer and can implement what security features they would like. With cloud systems this responsibility is in the hands of the vendor. With business controls and functions being accessible via the vendor's cloud ERP software, it is even more imperative that security assurances are given. A report by the Cloud Security Alliance in 2010 details some of the top security threats facing cloud systems[3].

A. Security Concerns And How The Are Combated

1) Threat #1:Malicious Abuse of Cloud Computing Services

More commonly with public cloud computing services, users can sign up anonymously for free or by using a valid payment method. This relative anonymity of the user is of advantage to people with the desire to disrupt the service. Hackers and people performing DDOS attacks, amongst other malicious actions can do so in relative ease. These actions can cause large disruption to innocent users of the service.

In an article published by ComputerWorld, the prevalence of DDOS attacks on cloud networks is highlighted[4]. Because a cloud computing network is a distributed system, an attack against a single user is in fact an attack against other users of this network. In order to combat this type of attack, the article suggests that cloud service providers need to ensure that they can differentiate between connections from innocent users and those of attackers. By doing so, the provider should then be able to take action to deal with the threat accordingly.

Other measures which can be taken include more stringent registration criteria in an attempt to screen against potential attackers. Additional network monitoring can be undertaken to try and detect potentially malicious network traffic as well as filtering against known blacklisted networks.

2) Threat #2:Threats From Internal Users

There are threats to security from employees of the cloud ERP providers. To a potential cloud service customer, the procedures and methods undertaken by the company when hiring a staff members are not clear. Because of this, customers are unable to make educated decisions on which provider to choose based on the recruitment policies and the likelihood of internal attacks. This lack of transparency could potentially mean that there is an ideal environment for reprisal attacks on the company. These attacks may be common from ex employees, but also from current ones too.

Depending on the access levels of the attacker, there is the potential for them to harvest confidential user information from the cloud. This can include business information too. This incident would be a major security breach and it is important for cloud ERP providers to take steps to combat this. Internally, there are several ways in which providers can counteract this threat. Many of these are procedures which can be undertaken to help prevent attacks. Companies can enforce compliance to a set of security and management practices which are frequently audited and reported upon in an attempt to reduce the risk. It is also advised that there is a breach response procedure in place to try and minimise any damage to the provider. For customers looking at purchasing an ERP system, it is advised that they conduct a strict supplier assessment to help identify and evaluate risk.

3) Threat #3: Data Leakage or Data Loss

To modern companies, data is paramount to their success and many steps are taken to ensure this data is safe. The data a company holds on contacts, suppliers and customers is extremely important to them. If this data was to be lost, due to poor data security procedures, the company would suffer greatly. Most companies have procedures in place to safeguard against data loss and to limit its effects. Routine backing up of data is a key part of such procedures, and the more regular the backup, the less the potential damage.

Loss of data isn't the only concern, there is another threat which can potentially cause more damage for a company in the long term. Leakage of data via careless data handling or from hacking can be a huge problem. The damaging after effects of such an incident are well documented in the case of Sony in 2011[5]. The data breach meant that 77 million users of Sony's PlayStation network had their user information, including passwords and usernames accessed by hackers. Breaches like this have been shown to damage customer confidence. A survey of 5,000 UK consumers in 2010 showed that 66% of customer would actively try to avoid companies who have had a data breach, and 17% of those questioned said they would never deal with the company again[6].

The LogRhythm research shows that it is important to ensure data security due to the potential massive loss in customer confidence and company credibility. The Cloud Security Alliance suggest some measures to take which can help limit damage. The use of encryption is a powerful method of protecting user data. Secure connections can be used between the client and the cloud service. For ERP customers, they can look to request data security practice information in order to make an informed decision on the ERP provider.

4) Threat #4:Physical Security Issues

Using a cloud ERP system for a business amongst other things, means that the company does not have to maintain and run ERP systems on computers in house. Instead, this pressure is taken off the company and passed to the ERP supplier. The computers running the ERP system need to be stored somewhere, and physical security measures should be taken in order to protect the cloud systems[8].

For companies using IT, physical security is a large part of the overall security plan. The phrase "a chain is only as strong as its weakest link" is one which is relevant in computer security. For example, a company could have the best firewall, network and server security preventing external hacker attacks. But this security is meaningless if a person with malicious intentions can simply walk into the server room unchallenged. This intruder then has physical access to where the cloud system is running and where data is stored. This is known as a physical security breach. If sufficient data practices are in place, then a physical breach does not need to mean that data is lost or compromised. Most commonly, the result is only service disruption.

There are many preventative measures which are taken by data centres to implement physical security. The most common being the installation of secure doors which accept door cards or codes which log access. Cameras can also be installed as a deterrent to potential intruders. Ensuring that all doors and windows are locked and opaque also add the overall security.

CONCLUSION

With the move to cloud computing comes security concerns. With an increasing number of companies moving to a cloud ERP system and more people using cloud services, the danger of attacks is increasing. It should be ensured that the great benefits of moving a business ERP system to the cloud don't cloud the importance of some decisions which need to be made to ensure success. The logistics of moving to a cloud ERP system and all other issues which this raises need to be considered, including security.

On the outset, it can look like moving to the cloud is an easy decision to make. This may be the case, but the security of business data needs to be ensured. As has been seen, security does not only relate to the cloud, but also where the cloud is physically located. High physical security is in place in many of these data centres. Threat #4 detailed some of the measures which should be taken to ensure security, and these measures should be investigated by businesses looking to use a cloud ERP system. Since a company's data is one of its most important assets, it is worth ensuring that moving it to a cloud service will still retain security.

Aside from physical security, there are a many threats which not only apply to cloud ERP systems, but cloud services in general. Threats from people seeking to disrupt services externally and internally are common. It has been seen how hackers can find it possible to hack into the systems of companies such as Sony with huge disruption in the short term, and customer confidence hits in the long term. For these reasons it is important that companies ensure that

their ERP providers are taking sufficient measures to prevent these type of attacks. Threats #1 and #2 show what can be done by providers to limit the possibility of attacks, and in the event of an attack, limit its damage. Procedures should be in place to deal which attacks and they should be reviewed in light of any fresh threats.

There are many IT security threats prevalent on the internet concerning personal users and businesses. With new technologies developing around the internet, it is important that security is of concern to the organisations affected. Problems can affect business, and with the online market being such a competitive arena, it is easy for consumers to use different companies for their needs. Detailed in this report are some basic measures that can be taken in order to ensure security to companies using ERP systems, the public looking to use the cloud and businesses seeking to be as competitive as possible.

REFERENCES

[1] Apple Inc, (2011). Press Info - Apple Introduces iCloud, [Online]. Available at: http://www.apple.com/pr/library/2011/06/06Apple-Introduces-iCloud.html. Accessed March 2012.

[2] P. Hoffman, (2008) ERP is Dead, Long Live ERP, [Online]. Available at: http://www.paulhofmann.net/wp-content/uploads/2011/01/ERP-Is-Dead-Long-Live-ERP.pdf. Accessed March 2012.

[3] Cloud Security Alliance, Top Threats to Cloud Computing v1.0, [Online] Available at: https://cloudsecurityalliance.org/topthreats/csathreats.v1.0.pdf. Accessed March 2012.

[4] Lohman. L, (2011). DDoS is Cloud's security Achilles heel, [Online]. Available at: http://www.computerworld.com.au/article/401127/ddos_cloud_achilles_heel. Accessed March 2012.

[5] ComputerWeekly, (2011). Sony data breach: 100m reasons to beef up security, [Online]. Available at: http://www.computerweekly.com/news/1280097348/Sony-data-breach-100m-reasons-to-beef-up-security. Accessed March 2012.

[6] LogRhythm, (2010). 80 percent of UK consumers support compulsory data loss disclosure, [Online]. Available at: http://logrhythm.com/Company/PressReleases/UKsupportscompulsorydatalossdisclosure.aspx. Accessed March 2012.

[7] Johnson. D, (2011). Security Issues in Cloud ERP, [Online]. Available at: http://erpcloudnews.com/2011/10/security-issues-in-cloud-erp/. Accessed March 2012.

[8] Johnson. D, (2011). Security Issues in Cloud ERP, [Online]. Available at: http://erpcloudnews.com/2011/10/security-issues-in-cloud-erp/. Accessed March 2012.

Implications and Prevention of Data Loss on Business utilising Cloud-based ERP Services

Charlie James Baker
School of Computing and Mathematics
University of Derby
Derby, United Kingdom
C.Baker2@unimail.derby.ac.uk

Abstract—**This document aims to explore the explosion of Cloud-based ERP services and their risks on data loss and provide recommendations of best practices to prevent data loss. Due to the explosion of Cloud-based ERP, the risk of data loss is increasing. Recommendations include implementing redundant layers of backup. (Abstract)**

Cloud;ERP; data loss; prevention (key words)

INTRODUCTION

With the advent of various service models such as Software-as-a-Service and the increasing popularity of Cloud-based services, many businesses are turning to these solutions for hosting their Enterprise Resource Planning systems. With more businesses turning to these solutions, they are relying more on being able to access their data 100% of the time. By not having direct control over their data and where it is stored they are introducing various risks and increasing the number of points of failure. This article considers the rise of Cloud systems and the effect of data loss on the businesses utilising them.

CLOUD AND ERP SYSTEMS

ERP or Enterprise Resource Planning systems are normally large systems within an enterprise or small business that are used to automate management of information across the organisation. These systems can be large, costly and incredibly time consuming to design, develop, test and implement.

Due to constraints with developing and implementing an in-house ERP system (even using existing off-the-shelf products) many businesses are turning to Cloud based ERP systems. This is also due to the rise in popularity of cloud or web based services. The "Cloud" has various definitions but in this case it means any system that is hosted externally and remotely accessed. They are run by various companies, the ERP system is basically outsourced to a remote company. Whilst existing in-house ERP systems have their own problems, utilising Cloud based systems to outsource business ERP to, brings its own set of problems, implications and consequences.

A. Examples

There are various cloud based ERP services available depending on what the business is looking for. Acumatica (http://www.acumatica.com) is one such company that provide Cloud ERP software. Some features include their own entire application suite, SaaS (Software as a Service) solutions which include all the hardware, upgrades and backups. Their software also supports running the entire system on the customer's own servers which just require a license. All of these features can considerably lower the costs and investment associated with an in-house system.

Another example is NetSuite (http://www.netsuite.co.uk) which includes web based accounting, real time inventory management and a complete customer relationship management.

As shown, these products can be extremely feature-rich. This furthers cloud based products as almost all required functions of the business are implemented already and could easily be used almost instantly after purchasing access to the product.

DISASTER STRIKES

Whilst all these features are good for the popularity and ease of use of Cloud based ERP systems, they come with their own set of problems. This set of problems includes issues such as Data Loss (and inability to access Data), Legal Issues and various other issues such as power failures.

In fact, Data issues account for the majority of the top ten ERP risks ranked by their mean of impact on the business. This table mentions incorrect data; confidential files access by unauthorised people; incomplete data within the top 5 ranks.

TABLE I. SOURCE: REFERENCE [3] PAGE 596, TABLE II

Rank	Risk item		Mean of impact (J)
1	OR1.2	Operational staff input incorrect data into the system	2.44
2	AR3.2	System fails to generate appropriate material net requirement plan	2.30
3	OWR4.5	Confidential data of the system is accessed by unauthorised people	2.29
4	OR3.2	ERP system contains inaccurate or incomplete bill of materials	2.28
5	OR3.3	ERP system contains inaccurate inventory records	2.27
5	AR3.1	Master production schedule generated by the ERP system is irrelevant	2.27
5	OWR1.1	Top managers make important IT decisions without consulting IT experts and system users	2.27
8	OWR2.1	IS/ERP plan is missing, ill-defined or misfit with business strategy	2.18
9	AR2.1	Sales forecast generated by ERP is inaccurate and inappropriate	2.17
10	OR2.2	Customer info files contained in ERP are out-of-date or incomplete	2.15

DATA: WHAT IS IT?

It is no secret that data is the main resource of a business to be able to function, but what is it exactly? Data could relate to many things but in this case Data is anything that is required for the business to function at the bare minimum. This includes the software to run the systems; the actual information that is stored such as customer records, invoices, employee records; process workflows and procedures; as well as non-data specific stuff such as tacit knowledge.

DATA LOSS: CAUSES

There are many reasons that data loss can occur. The following are the main causes of data loss with a brief explanation of each.

A. Loss of Access

There are many reasons why businesses may end up with loss of access to their valuable data such as legal reasons. The operator may end up being shut down and raided with the business' data being taken away when the servers are confiscated. This is a more extreme example but it could also be something simple such as a switch going offline or a UPS failing.

B. No Backups / Insufficient Redundancy

One of the big mistakes is not having any backups. Along with having no backups, a big mistake if housing all the backups in one location. Storing business ERP in the cloud may result in backups being made by the service, or they may not. This could vary by service. The business should make their own backups and store them offsite to their location, as well as the location of the ERP system in the event of natural disaster or not (such as fire).

C. Poor Policy Enforcement

Whilst Policy is meant to be adhered to, there are inevitably cases where policy is simply ignored or the importance of policy isn't stressed enough to personnel. This can have catastrophic consequences if certain actions are not correctly undertaken. A simple example of this would be the person responsible for producing the daily backups failing to complete this task. This could ultimately result in adequate backups not existing in the event of a disaster

D. System Mismatches

Different systems must work together in a business. This is especially important when new systems are implemented and must interface with legacy systems. System mismatches can inevitably cause something to go wrong and cause data to be lost in transit

E. Multiple Process Workflows

Process Workflows can help with enforcing policy. Conflicting process workflows however may not. Multiple workflows will encourage conflicting steps to occur which – although not by themselves – may aid in the spiral to catastrophic failure.

F. Summary

All of these are reasons that can aid in catastrophic failure as well as cause them. There are a number of end results of catastrophic failure such as hardware failure. The main one however is data loss. Data is the heart of almost every business in existence. Without data the business would fail to function and could easily send the business back to day 1.

PREVENTION

There are a number of ways to prevent data loss. The most popular way is called Redundancy.

A. Redundancy

Redundancy is the duplication of mission critical components or functions of a system. This allows the business to have multiple ways to access the data. Examples include having multiple copies of backups or even having multiple backups in multiple locations in case of catastrophic failure.

The main method of preventing these issues with data loss is to provide redundant systems for backup purposes. Duplicate machines may be implemented at the provider level (in this case, the cloud-based ERP service) but they may also be run at the business level alongside the existing system as an alternative should the worst scenario begin to play out. Other methods of redundancy implementation include having multiple internet connections in case of failure, especially in the case that all of the business' data is stored in the cloud. An even better way would include running your own local servers with the same software provided by the Cloud-based ERP service as another layer of protection. Most Cloud-based ERP services provide this functionality – although at an extra cost for the licenses and hardware.

Redundancy is also more than just backed up data. It also includes having adequate numbers of staff with access to tacit knowledge available in case of inevitable events such as death. Other related items that should be implement some type of redundancy include documentation, process workflows and procedures – electronic and physical in case of loss

B. Reconstruction

An additional approach is by utilising data provenance. Data provenance is historic information that is stored about data that can be used to track its history such as changes made including which changes; who changed it and most importantly when the files was changed. Utilising data provenance we could create historic backups of files at set intervals (daily, weekly, etc.) and use this information to reconstruct files in the event of a corrupted file or data loss. This would require that the file information be stored separately but this should be done anyway for multiple reasons already stated.

Data provenance would be especially useful in the event of a data loss disaster as it could be possibly to piece together the remainder of files which could lead to data recovery or to find the culprit of the incident.

CONCLUSION

Cloud-based ERP systems are growing in popularity due to the boom of "The Cloud" and the rising costs of implementing in-house ERP systems. This is also due to costs being much less versus rolling out in-house systems. Whilst Cloud based systems are great for efficiency, maintainability they introduce their own set of risks.

These risks include loss of data; loss of access to data as well as security issues such as theft of data or legal issues. Many of the risks could be triggered by a simple switch failing, causing the business to lose access to their data.

Loss of access to data can be extremely devastating to businesses. Businesses may be relying on a particular service without any fallbacks.

To mitigate these problems, this paper recommends that redundant systems are implemented at either the service level or down at the business level. Preferably at the business level as they can then control where their data goes, such as to multiple cloud ERP services. This can also be accomplished by the Cloud provider implementing redundant systems to make sure that downtime in relation to access of data is minimal – if they haven't already. Businesses may also wish to run the software on their own systems as an in-house "cloud" which they can use in event of catastrophic failure. A proper backup operating procedure should be implemented to mitigate the risk of any data loss as well as loss of access to data and their relating risks.

REFERENCES

[1] Huang, S., 2004, Assessing risk in ERP projects: identify and prioritize the factors. Industrial Management & Data Systems, Volume 104 Issue 8, Pages 681 – 688. [Online]

[2] Xu H., 2002, Data quality issues in implementing an ERP. Industrial Management & Data Systems, Volume 102 Issue 1, Pages 47 – 58. [Online]

[3] Peng G.C., Nunes M.B., 2009, Identification and assessment of risks associated with ERP post-implementation in China. Journal of Enterprise Information Management, Volume 22 Issue 5, Pages 587 – 614. [Online]

[4] Ifinedo, P., 2008, Impacts of business vision, top management support, and external expertise on ERP success. Business Process Management Journal, Volume 14 Issue 4, Pages 551 – 568. [Online]

[5] Scott, J.E., 2002, Managing Risks in Enterprise Systems Implementations. Communications of the ACM. Volume 34 Issue 4, Pages 74-81. [Online]

Evaluation of the Risk of SaaS ERP Solutions within SME's

Dominic Davies-Tagg
University of Derby
100076940@unimail.derby.ac.uk

Abstract –Software as a Service is steadily becoming a viable ERP option for Small/Medium Enterprises, with lower upfront costs and benefits such as rapid deployment, increased user adoption and reduced support. But just as an On-Premise ERP system has risk a Cloud based SaaS solution has its own unique risks. Within this report the potential risks of utilizing a SaaS ERP solution are addressed and evaluated within the context of SME's who are at present the target market.

Keywords: SaaS; ERP; Cloud; SME's; Risk;

BACKGROUND

A. About SaaS and the importance of risk evaluation

SaaS (Software-as-a-Service) is a hosting model for ERP (Enterprise Resource Planning) software; it involves a company's ERP solution on a vendor's servers. This model provides a variety benefits such as: Simple Deployment, reduced initial ERP cost, reduced in-house tech support and maintenance work conducted by vendor.

The SaaS model is relatively new and uptake continues to grow [1], but awareness of the risks associated with implementing a SaaS ERP is low, so it is important to identify and evaluate the potential risks to increase awareness on the subject.

B. Importance of SME's

SME's make up 99.9% of businesses within the UK [2] so are of particular importance, considering the present economic situation and that in past recessions it has been SME's that have brought us out of economic trouble [2].

SME's are currently the target users of SaaS services due to the affordability SaaS offers over the high up-front costs of on-site ERP [3].

INVESTIGATION

In this report the term "risk" is used, but some items are better defined as a threat or vulnerability.

The risks to be evaluated have been split into four specific categories that best suit the risk.

A. Security Risk

Security is a big concern regardless of business size or ERP implementation, but SaaS introduces the vendor to the equation enabling new risks.

SaaS systems are located with the vendor, meaning that all data is also stored with them depending on the type of business the data could be a company's most valuable asset and a business could potentially stop operations without it [4].

If the business had the servers on-site they would know that they were safe and secure, with backup and recovery solutions in place in the event of disaster, but how does the company know the SaaS vendor provides an adequate level of safety with data they are storing.

SLA's (Service Level Agreements) are commonly agreed with the SaaS vendor, covering backups, recovery, physical security and digital security. But SaaS vendors have not been forthcoming in how such protocols are actually actioned [5], so can vendors be trusted to honour SLA's to the standard that was defined and is expected. When signing and agreeing to an SLA it is important to be aware of the current/future potential threats as technology rapidly advances vendors may not cover you against these emerging threats [5] and safety concerns.

SaaS ERP solutions are provided across the internet, but at present is the internet a safe place to be keeping potentially sensitive data especially in light of the increasing number of hacking of websites and data theft [6].

The most unexpected risk but potentially damaging can come from the vendor, just as a business places value on its data the vendor might also see the value of the data it holds leading to unscrupulous activities like the selling of data, these risks could arise from ambiguities/loopholes in the contract with the vendor [7] or the vendor could be conducting themselves in an illegal manner and stealing your data. So it is important SME's choose a respected vendor and conduct plenty of research before agreeing to any contracts.

B. Economic Risk

The initial cost of implementing a SaaS solution may be cheaper than an on-site hosted solution and doesn't have the all the on-going maintenance and support employee costs but it needs to be considered that SaaS is a service that is provided to the SME and like all services extra charges commonly exist, only being encountered at a much later date in the contract.

The risk of these extra charges is likely to occur when change is required; this could be increasing the size of the data the business has access to, alterations to the service due to restructuring within a business or even changing SaaS vendors. The swapping of vendors can be highly costly mainly due to them not wanting to lose custom and is a resource intensive activity, so vendors could charge heavily for the change.

Hidden charges can exist similar to when a mobile phone usage plan is exceeded, what if the service plan the business is currently subscribed to has used up all of its allotted space/resources, a business can't just stop the ERP from operating as it will be a mission critical part of the organisation [8] so realistically businesses end up paying the price no matter how inflated, as its more important to keep the business operating, especially with a smaller business with fewer customers as if they lose faith in the business, contracts that are sustaining the business could be lost.

The vendor also has a huge amount of bargaining power concerning the amount charged for services, as they hold all of a business's data [9]. A larger company may challenge this sort of practice by taking the vendor to court but being a smaller company it may prove less damaging to pay the inflated prices and continue business operations than to undergo a pricey legal battle.

C. Performance Risk

When change occurs within the software solutions that a business uses it can be to address new legal requirements or that the licensing on old software has changed but commonly greater performance will be a business's driving factor for change.

The risk exists that the anticipated/advertised availability, network bandwidth, speed and overall performance is not delivered by a SaaS solution [10]. These performance problems can come from a variety of places, it could be the service that the vendor is providing or the internet speed used, it could also be on the businesses own side that the internet connection cannot support the SaaS well enough or interface with existing solutions.

Existing home-grown applications may be fundamental to the success of a business and will often be finely tuned for performance but if SaaS solution isn't interoperable with these applications a huge risk exists of having to either develop new applications or endure the performance provided by poor compatibility [11].

As mentioned within Economic risk, downtime can impact heavily on a smaller business and affect its reputation if customer facing services are affected and if day to day procedures are not supported correctly, resulting in loss of revenues and potentially customers [12].

Large big business companies can easily address these risks, for example if they need better internet speed it is entirely viable for them to roll out fast fibre as needed, or change internal infrastructures swiftly and efficiently without detriment to the business. But SME's do not have this luxury and have to endure with poor performance until it becomes viable to secure changes to rectify the performance issues [13].

D. Strategic Risk

Strategic risk is the loss of critical resources and capabilities when sending applications to a SaaS alternative.

Putting everything into SaaS creates a huge level of dependence on the vendor and this is something you do not

want [14]. When a business is choosing a SaaS solution and wants to implement it they need to consider the potential of the SaaS provider having some major incident and losing all of a company's data, with this in mind do all of the business processes need to be migrated to the SaaS Cloud or can some processes remain internally to give the business certain measures against total disaster and control over some of their own infrastructure [14].

One of the advantages of being a smaller company is that you can adapt to change in industries quickly unlike huge enterprises [12], but without full control over your ERP system you can lose this advantage as by the time change is negotiated and implemented in coordination with your vendor the industry could be changing again.

CONCLUSION

A. Key risks identified for SME's

Unfortunately the material covered here gives the impression that the vendor is the key source of risk for SaaS implementations but many vendors will be upstanding and offer the highest service quality possible, regardless of this it is the vendor who holds all of the businesses data and holds a position of power over the business, potential exists for the vendor to conduct illegal/unscrupulous activities [7], so it is better to be aware of the potential risk that vendors can and do impose.

Security of data is a major concern for any business, but SME's with a smaller customer base have potentially a lot more to lose if a security problem occurs and customer data is leaked or stolen, losing several big customers over an issue like this could result in the end of a business. So businesses need to consider should something potentially ruining be located with a third party.

B. Recommending a SaaS ERP solution

Even though this report has only addressed risk and the negative side of a SaaS solution I believe that SaaS is still perfect for SME's to access ERP solutions and enhance their business. But this relies on a safe and trusting relationship being made between the business and the vendor, instead of a service provider to customer relationship a closer business partnership should be made so that the business and vendor work in unison to ensure that everyone is happy with the service delivered [12].

SME's should consider choosing a SaaS ERP system but should take time in deciding and researching who the vendor they plan to utilize is and their past successes, only implementing what is necessary within the SaaS ERP keeping as many mission critical systems back as possible to maintain control over aspects of your own infrastructure and finally thinking forward to potential business expansion in relation to additional expenses that may be incurred.

C. To the Future

SaaS solutions were once delivered by only small start-up ventures but today even big companies such as Oracle and SAP are joining the SaaS market and providing their services to the world, these companies invoke a level of trust that you cannot get from smaller vendors so many of the concerns and risk with vendors may be addressed by these huge companies making SaaS less risky than if you hosted it yourself utilizing there many years of expertise.

REFERENCES

[1] R. Wong, "Comparing The ROI of SaaS Versus On-Premise Using Forrester's TEI Apprach", Forrester Research Inc., September 20, 2009.

[2] BERR, "Small and Mediun Sized Enterprises (SME) Statistics for the UK", Methodology and Accuracy Technical Note, Enterprise Directorate, 2006.-

[3] T. Haselmann, G. Vossen, "Software –as-a-service in small and medium enterprises: an empricial attitude assessment, WISE'11 Proceedings of the 12ᵗʰ international conference on web information systems engineering, springer-verlag, Heidelberg, Berlin, 2011.

[4] J. Jurison, "The Role of risk and return in information technology outsourcing decisions", Journal of Information Technology, Vol. 10, Issue 4, pp. 239-247, 1995.

[5] O. Hart, "Incomplete contracts and the theory of the firm", Journal of Law, Economics & Organization, Vol. 4, Issue 1, pp. 119-139, 1988.

[6] P. Carroll, "Standards of data protection", Computer Fraud & Security, Vol 2012, Issue 2, pp. 5-7, 2012.

[7] L. Wilcocks, G. Fitzgerald, "Market as opportunity? Case studies in outsourcing information technology and services", The Journal of Strategic Information Systems, Vol. 2, Issue. 3, pp. 223-242, 1993.

[8] J. Barthelemy, "The hidden costs of IT outsourcing", Sloan Management Review, Vol 42, Issue 3, pp.60-69, 2001.

[9] M. Xin, N. Levina, "Software-as-a-service model: elaborating client-side adoption factors", Proceeds of the Twenty-Ninth International Conference on Information Systems, Paper 86, Paris, France, 2008.

[10] H. Gewald, J. Dibbern, "Risks and benefits of business process outsourcing: a study of transaction services in the German banking industry", Information and Management , Vol. 46, Issue. 4, pp. 249–257, 2009.

[11] T. Dillion, W. Chen, E. Chang, "Cloud Computing: Issues and Challenges", Advanced Information Networking and Applications (AINA), 2010 24ᵗʰ IEEE International Conference , Perth, pp. 27-33, 2010.

[12] A. Benlian, T. Hess, "Opportunities and risks of software-as-a-service: Findings from a survey of IT executives", Decision Support Systems, Vol. 52, pp. 232-246, 2011.

[13] D. Zielinski, "Be Clear on Cloud Computing Contracts", HRMagazine, 2009.

[14] T. Kern, J. Kreijger, L. Willcocks, "Exploring ASP as sourcing strategy: theoretical perspectives, propositions for practice", The Journal of Strategic Information Systems, Vol. 11, Issue. 2, pp. 153–177, 2002.

Application Wrapping: Accessing Legacy ERP Applications on Mobile Devices

Dimitar Kokov

University of Derby

Derby, United Kingdom

d.kokov1@unimail.derby.ac.uk

Abstract—**Although modern mobile devices are starting to substitute desktop computers for activities such as email communication and web browsing, there are accessibility issues that prevent them from being used more often in the enterprise. The paper discusses those issues with regards to desktop and web-based legacy applications and analyses the available solutions based on non-invasive re-engineering techniques (application wrapping). As a result of those techniques, the legacy applications are transformed into either web applications or web services. It has been concluded that despite resolving the accessibility issues, the outcome of each approach in general is a software solution with relatively slow response rates. A significant advantage on the other hand is the opportunity to easily integrate the "wrapped" legacy applications with other ERP applications in future.**

Keywords-application wrapping; legacy applications; accessibility issues; web-based applications; desktop applications; web services.

INTRODUCTION

With the continuous technological advancement and the development of smaller and more powerful computer chips, mobile devices are now able to perform most computing activities of an average desktop or laptop user - web browsing, email communication, multimedia interaction etc. This has allowed business professionals to become more flexible, active, informed and approachable. Having realized those benefits, companies have started to develop and/or adapt their enterprise resource planning (ERP) systems for both desktop and mobile devices [1].

The aim of this paper is to point out some of the common issues of and approaches to enabling legacy ERP applications on mobile devices. Since legacy applications might be costly or difficult to re-build, another adaptation approach is required. The solutions proposed in this paper defer depending on the architecture of each legacy application, but are all based on the application wrapping technique.

The term "mobile devices" is used to generalize small hand-held devices such as cell phones, PDAs and tablets, but does not include netbook and laptop computers.

ACCESSIBILITY ISSUES

Legacy applications can be divided into two groups based on their architecture: web applications and client-server (desktop) applications. Since desktop applications require custom clients, a major issue can be the costly or even impossible, due to unavailable source code, development of a mobile client application [2]. Furthermore, the fast advancement of mobile devices can result in the application not being supported on newer models, thus requiring another investment in newer software.

Web legacy applications, on the other hand, are accessed through a web browser instead of specific client software and since most modern mobile devices have a preinstalled web browser, theoretically there should not be any accessibility issues. However, due to the limited memory and processing power of those devices, only a small number of web standards are supported, leaving web applications developed with proprietary technologies - such as Flash and Java – inaccessible [2]. Nevertheless, the small bandwidth and screen size of mobile devices make it difficult to display and navigate web applications developed for desktop use, even if the web technology/standard is supported [2]. TABLE III. summarizes the accessibility issues mentioned above.

TABLE III.   ACCESSIBILITY ISSUES

Issues with accessing legacy systems on mobile devices	
Desktop legacy applications	*Web legacy applications*
Need of custom client application for each type of mobile device	Limited support for web standards and proprietary vendors
Low processing power	
Low memory	
Small/Limited bandwidth	
Small screen size	

THE CONCEPT OF APPLICATION WRAPPING

In order to address the issues from the previous section, legacy systems need to be re-engineered. The re-engineering approach can be divided into two groups of techniques – invasive and non-invasive [3]. The former involves modifications to the software and is often subject to the availability of the source code. The latter requires the development of middleware software which interacts with the legacy application without altering its program code. It functions by "wrapping" around the application and "translating" incoming requests and outgoing responses, enabling users to access the natively unsupported application [3]. Figure 2 below illustrates the application wrapping architecture.

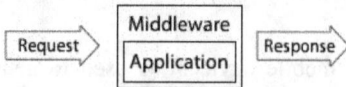

Figure 2. Application wrapping architecture

Some of the major reasons for using a non-invasive approach are:

- The legacy application is developed by an external company and the source code is unavailable.

- The legacy application has to be accessed through a new medium while keeping the original version running for its initial purpose.

- The legacy application is written in an obsolete programming language, which lacks functionality.

- The complete re-development of the legacy application is expensive and/or will take too long.

The following sections discuss how the concept of application wrapping is applied for both desktop and web legacy applications, so that they can be accessed on mobile devices.

WRAPPING DESKTOP APPLICATIONS

The transformation mechanism, depicted on Figure 3, includes a client application (web browser), a web server and an Application Migration Solution (AMS) server [4]. The client communicates with the webserver, which transfers the request to the AMS server. There, the legacy application driver extracts the parameters from the request and feeds them into the legacy application. The response is then "scanned" by a GUI Recognition tool, which separates data from interface controls and transmits them both to the web server. Based on the user interface (UI) type that the GUI Recognition tool has sent, the web server loads a corresponding HTML template from a library of precompiled templates for each UI type of the legacy application. The template is then combined with the actual

response data from the AMS server and sent back to the client in the form of HTML pages.

Since the initially generated templates are entirely written in standard HTML without the use of vendor specific technologies, mobile devices will be able to display them successfully. Furthermore, the approach gives the opportunity to generate different templates for different screen sizes – i.e. for mobile phones and for tablets. The library of templates also makes it easier to alter the look and feel of the application

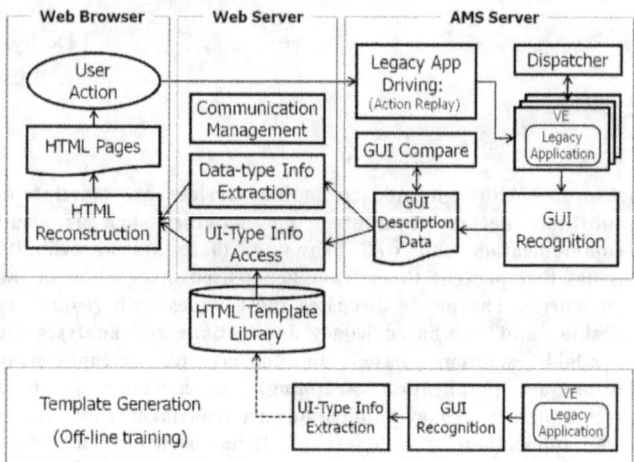

Figure 3. Desktop application wrapped into web application

without changing its code, making it up to date with modern design best practices and user preferences. Another significant advantage, derived from the separation of data and user interface, is that by wrapping the legacy application for web access it also becomes easily integrated with other applications [4]. The response data alone can be sent to other ERP applications, since applications do not need GUIs to communicate with each other.

Despite the positive sides of application wrapping, it has some disadvantages as well. Although the use of HTML templates allows caching and response messages are relatively small [4], this approach in general suffers from performance issues. The bigger amount of messages transmitted between the three tiers and the long sequence of operations in the AMS server make the application considerably slow. Therefore, the physical location, connectivity and load of the Web and AMS servers play a significant role and need to be considered carefully in order to achieve the optimal speed performance.

WRAPPING WEB APPLICATIONS

Although modern mobile devices have web browsers, some web applications might be inaccessible or might display incorrectly [1]. In case the issues are the small screen size and the limited bandwidth of the mobile device, the standard HTML and Cascading Style Sheets (CSS) technologies can be used to resolve the issue, since they are widely supported [5]. The general purpose of HTML is to program the structure and interface controls of webpages, while CSS is used to describe their presentation. Assuming that the legacy web application has been developed following those guidelines, the adaptation to mobile devices can be achieved by developing a separate CSS file for presentation on smaller screen sizes [5]. The application is than wrapped into a driver which checks the user agent of each client and redirects the request to the appropriate CSS file. This way the actual application remains intact and its design is changed only for mobile device users.

If, on the other hand, HTML and CSS codes are not entirely separated in the legacy application, another approach is required. Figure 4 illustrates the architecture of a web application turned into a collection of web services. Each function of the application is represented as a sequence of actions that need to be executed, along with certain input and output data [6]. This information forms each automaton and is stored into the automaton repository. Once a web service is initiated, the Automaton Interpreter invokes the corresponding automaton, loads the input data and interconnects it with the Web Application Interaction module, which sends an HTTP request to the application. The same module then parses the HTTP response and extracts the desired data from the webpage. Finally, the output data is transmitted.

To make the application accessible on mobile devices, a web-based interface will be needed for each web service [6]. This leaves the impression that a whole new application is developed instead of just adding a new interaction layer to the legacy application. Similarly to the application wrapping technique from the previous section, this approach significantly affects the performance of the wrapped version of the application. In contrast, the availability of a web service for each feature of the legacy application can serve as means for direct integration to other ERP applications. Furthermore, it shifts the architecture to service oriented (SOA), allowing the company to benefit from the advantages of SOA [7].

Other web legacy applications, which are often inaccessible on mobile devices, are those written in resource-demanding and/or non-standard client-side programming languages and those that incorporate vendor-specific technologies – i.e. Flash, Java applets, complex JavaScript code etc. The actual issue in the case of Java and Flash web applications is that the programming code remains hidden from the client. Therefore it cannot be parsed as in the previous solution. Taking those limitations into consideration, a suitable solution can be the first approach (Figure 3), but implemented for a web-based application, because it does not require access to the programming code. Since the legacy application is hosted on a web-server, the AMS can also be hosted on the same server, reducing request/response messages. Therefore the solution should have better response times compared to the one from section 0.

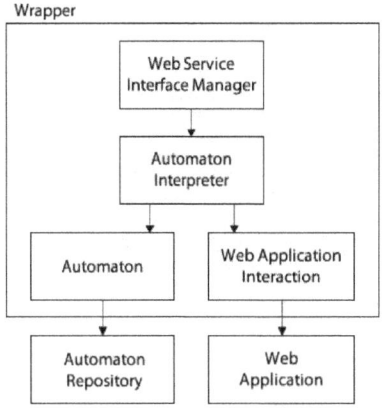

Figure 4. Web application turned into web services

CONCLUSIONS AND FUTURE WORK

After analysing the accessibility issues that prevent the use of legacy applications on mobile devices, the paper has proposed solutions to the problem for both desktop and web-based legacy systems. In theory, the discussed approaches can be successfully applied to virtually any type of application. But they are by no means always the most appropriate or rational solution. A positive side effect that can be achieved by application wrapping is that it enables a potential communication channel which can be used for future integration and interconnection purposes.

The application wrapping approach proposed at the end of section 0 is based on theoretical assumptions. In future work, it will be experimentally tested in order to form an implementation methodology for those particular type of legacy applications.

REFERENCES

[1] Goth, G.; , "Mobile devices present integration challenges," IT Professional , vol.1, no.3, pp.11-15, May/Jun 1999

[2] Stormer, H. "Exploring Solutions for a MobileWeb", E-Commerce Technology, 2006. The 8th IEEE International Conference on and Enterprise Computing, E-Commerce, and E-Services, The 3rd IEEE International Conference on , pp.75, 26-29 June 2006

[3] El-Ramley, M., Stroulia, E., Samir, H. "Legacy Systems Interaction Reengineering", Human-Centered Software Engineering, Human-Computer Interaction Series, p. 316, 2009

[4] Xin Meng; Jingwei Shi; Xiaowei Liu; Huifeng Liu; Lian Wang; , "Legacy Application Migration to Cloud," Cloud Computing (CLOUD), 2011 IEEE International Conference on , pp.750-751, 4-9 July 2011

[5] Guirguis, S.K.; Hassan, M.A.; , "A smart framework for web content and resources adaptation in mobile devices," Advanced Communication Technology (ICACT), 2010 The 12th International Conference on , vol.1, pp.487-492, 7-10 Feb. 2010

[6] Di Lorenzo, G.; Fasolino, A.R.; Melcarne, L.; Tramontana, P.; Vittorini, V.; , "Turning Web Applications into Web Services by Wrapping Techniques," Reverse Engineering, 2007. WCRE 2007. 14th Working Conference on , pp.199-208, 28-31 Oct. 2007

[7] Kryvinska, N.; Strauss, C.; Auer, L.; , "Next Generation Applications Mobility Management with SOA - A Scenario-Based Analysis," Complex, Intelligent and Software Intensive Systems (CISIS), 2010 International Conference on , pp.415-420, 15-18 Feb. 2010

Critical success factors in the implementation of Cloud-based ERP systems

Vivianne Tay Hui Yen
School of Computing and Mathematics
University of Derby
Derby, United Kingdom
100240712@unimail.derby.ac.uk

Abstract—ERP systems have been an important tool within an organization as they can integrate business processes and functions as a whole. However, 65% of executives consider that ERP systems adversely will affect the business processes due to the potential for implementation problems. Therefore, four critical success factors (CSF) are examined to determine whether the implementation will be successful. This paper identifies top management commitment, business process re-engineering, IT infrastructure, and change management as key factors. Investigations on key features of cloud-based ERP system have been discussed. Comparison between traditional ERP systems and cloud-based systems shows that cloud-based ERP systems bring benefits to enterprises. Strategies for making decisions are examined to adopt a cloud-based ERP system in the conclusion.

Keywords-ERP systems; implementation; cloud; critical success factors

BACKGROUND

"*ERP systems are said to be the umbrella for integrating sets of business applications that allow an enterprise to manage and control almost all aspects of functions.*" [2]. A successful ERP system is important as it can affect the whole business processes of an organisation. ERP systems can be complicated. Almost 50% of ERP implementations prove to be unsuccessful because of budgeting and lack of focus within the business process and change management, and hence, fail to achieve the objectives of the enterprise [2]. In order to handle all of the problems which lead to the failures of ERP implementation, it is crucial for an organisation to understand the critical success factors of ERP system implementation. Critical success factors (CSF) are important because they can determine which of the factors are most influential in the process of implementing an ERP system so that decision making can be improved and failure rates can be decreased [9]. Among all of the critical success factors, there are four main factors that have a huge impact in implementing an ERP system, namely: Top management commitment, Business process re-engineering, IT infrastructure, and Change management.

A. Top management commitment

In order to implement a successful ERP system, top management support is a crucial success factor because the decision made by the management can determine whether enough resources are made available to support an ERP system or not. ERP projects often fail during implementation. The main reason is because senior management delegate the responsibility to the technology department which would put the entire company's survival at risk [1]. The roles of top management are to develop a perception of the capabilities and limitations of IT, set up reasonable objectives for IT systems, reveal strong obligation to the successful prologue of IT and more. Hence, without the support of top management, an ERP system might face failure half way or could not be completed. Therefore, the importance of top management's participation should be highlighted in the implementation of an ERP system due to it being an expensive and time-consuming task.

B. Business process re-engineering

It is often said that reengineering the existing business process is important to achieve the "best business process standard" when implementing an ERP system [1]. The alignment between the business processes and the ERP system is crucial to meet the greatest advantage provided in an ERP system [9]. There are only 70% of the organisational needs that can be met when installing the best application package [2]. A package installed is important to match with the business processes in an organisation, or else, the total cost of implementation will be increased as more customisation is needed [1]. Hence, it is imperative to reengineer the business process instead of customising the software as it can reduce the costs needed in implementation.

C. Information Technology (IT) Infrastructure

Adequate hardware and networking infrastructure are critical during the ERP implementation [2]. Furthermore, the software configuration presents a huge impact on the implementation procedure and consequences. The functions of an ERP system depend on an effective IT infrastructure in order to succeed in the eventual installation.

D. Change management

The main problem faced by ERP systems is due to managers underestimating the impact of changes in the implementation, because it might change the way an organisation operates. *"Training and education is an important process in change management."*[5] During the process of development and implementation of an ERP system, the involvement of users is very important to understand the overall concept of the system and the effects on business processes [4]. It is critical that users can be prepared to use the new system to avoid confusion [5]. A proper change management effort is essential to be carried out. However, implementing a traditional ERP system is different from implementing a cloud-based ERP system. Hence, factors which drive the adoption of ERP system in the clouds will now be explored to determine the differences.

INVESTIGATION

E.   Key features of Cloud based ERP

"Cloud computing is one of the most discussed technologies in recent years. Interest in cloud computing is mainly motivated by its potential to reduce capital expenditures and to deliver scalable IT services at lower variable costs." [8] The term "cloud" is an idea to increase the accessibility of the daily business processes in an organisation and also ensure the flexibility of users to access any applications from anywhere at anytime with an internet-based connection [3]. There are four critical factors which are cost, flexibility, scalability and autonomic which drive the adoption of cloud computing services [8].

1.   Flexibility

Some of the professional network companies such as Google and IBM set up "Cloud Computing" as a computer storage centre which makes "Cloud" storage of material and application services [8]. High-speed infrastructure like telecommunications and network technology have been progressing rapidly which ensures the availability and convenience of the accessibility of large quantity of software applications. Moreover, processing and sharing of information can be achieved, as all of the data can be found online which makes cloud-based ERP systems different from traditional ERP systems. The process of installing complex systems can be ignored as an organisation can fully utilise the usage of the wireless networks for the purpose of data transmission. Hence, real time information is available and can be obtained immediately throughout the internet as an integrated Information System (IS).

2.   Low capital investment

"Cloud computing is well known as a web service interface to operating system virtualization."[7] Software-as-a-Service (SaaS) is a software model which allows users to get the services from the internet without the need to invest massively in neither IT infrastructure nor software. Compared to the traditional on-premise software model, the Software-as-a-Service (SaaS) software model offers low initial cost. Maintenance, operation and subscription costs are either low or can be reduced because all of the functions, upgrading and operations of the systems are maintained by the service provider which helps an enterprise to save IT resources during the phase from development to implementation. Hence, this

model provides predetermined financial and operative advantages which enabling the enterprise to alter their business processes and therefore helping the organisation to achieve high performance of IT services with lower cost in implementation.

3.   Scalability

Unlike traditional ERP system, *"The cloud is a concept of virtualization of resources that maintains and manages itself in which processing and storage are not physically present at the user's location."* [7] All of the applications and servers are accessible through the internet. The major difference between the traditional and cloud-based ERP system is that the cloud-based ERP system has the ability of the system to manage an increment in the complexity of additional resources while there is a limited flexibility to scale the resources in the traditional ERP system [6]. Thus, the availability of application and software can be ensure and hence guarantee the service level.

4.   Autonomic

In addition, cloud-based ERP system can reduce the burden of IT engineers as service providers needs to deal with all the software so that the IT engineers can focus mainly on the core business [7]. The overall IT standard can be enhanced as large-scale construction can be accomplished throughout the procedure optimisation [7]. The behaviour autonomic services enhance the productivity of the organisation in improving the quality of services, security and fault-tolerance [6].

COMPARING CLOUD-BASED ERP WITH TRADITIONAL ERP

A.   A comparison of CSF for traditional system vs. cloud-based ERP system

The table below explained the comparison between the traditional and cloud-based ERP system. IT infrastructure can be ignored once cloud-based ERP system is implemented. However, the other three factors are still the CSF to implement a cloud-based ERP system successfully. Cloud-based ERP system helped organisation in saving cost and time as ERP system had been a real expensive and time-consuming task. Effective and productive services can be achieved by implementing a cloud-based ERP system in an organisation.

TABLE IV.   COMPARISON OF CSF BETWEEN TRADITIONAL SYSTEM AND CLOUD-BASED ERP SYSTEM

Critical Success Factors	Traditional ERP System	Cloud-based ERP system
Top management commitment	Support from top management is critical as ERP system implementation is a lengthy, complicated and challenges task to be implemented in an organisation.	It is important to have the support of top management as their main role is to provide sufficient resources and clear direction to implement a system successfully.

Critical Success Factors	Traditional ERP System	Cloud-based ERP system
Business process re-engineering	Re-engineering business process is critical during the implementation of ERP system to meet organisation's needs because cost will be higher if customisation of software is needed within an enterprise.	Business processes should represent the business services in an organisation. In order to improve the performance of the organisation, re-structuring the business processes is important to achieve objectives of the organisation.
IT infrastructure	Sufficient and adequate hardware and network will need to be installed and functioning well to be parallel with the current business processes.	Everything can be done via internet; therefore, IT infrastructure can be ignored during the implementation of cloud-based ERP system.
Change management	More education and training will need to be done for users to be more knowledgeable to manage the functions of ERP system as business processes will need to be reengineering in order to have a successful ERP system.	Users needed to be trained to understand the overall concept of cloud-based ERP to avoid chaos so that users can acknowledge the advantages of implementing a cloud-based ERP system and adapt to the new system in an organisation.

CONCLUSION

A. *Strategies for making decisions about adopting cloud ERP*

ERP systems are multifaceted system so strategies are needed to move towards cloud-based system. Throughout development, the connection of application and business processes is the main issue of concerned. Therefore, a technology-organisation-environment (TOE) framework is feasible to be applied as a strategy to investigate the IT adoption by firms. *"The technological context refers to internal and external technologies in a firm while the organisational context refers to the firm size, centralisation, formalisation, and more. Additionally, the environment context refers to a firm's industry and competitors."* [3]

1. *Technology context*

"Cloud computing services, which allow operations to be generalised and mobilised through internet transactions, can substitute for or complement ERP software."[3] The reason of why technology should be considered because cloud computing services can enhance the speed of business communications, provide efficient coordination, boost communication and improve the accessibility to market. [3] Alternatively, cloud-based systems can be new to users who might be unfamiliar and may have a lack of confidence in the system. Therefore, users may need to take time to understand the new system. In addition, it is essential for the technology to be compatible with the application systems as an organisation will consider adopting new technology if there is no adjustment in processes needed to be made.

2. *Organisational context*

Furthermore, top management plays a significant role in the adoption of cloud-based ERP system as the integration of resources and re-engineering business processes may evolve during the implementation. With the aid of them, a clearer goal and vision can be developed to create a positive environment as complexities of technologies are growing drastically. Subsequently, firm size is one of the major determinants during implementation as small firms are likely to adopt less innovation due to the limited flexibility and ability of risk taking within an enterprise. Additionally, technological readiness is one of the critical points in implementing a cloud-based ERP system because new network technologies and applications are built and users will need to have adequate knowledge and skills about it.

3. *Environmental context*

Last but not least, rapid changes in high-tech industries have influenced many organisations facing different types of pressures. They are aware of their competitor's activities such as installing or upgrading into a new system. Benefits such as better understanding of market visibility, the efficiency of operation can be increased and real time data can be collected accurately can be achieved by adopting cloud-based ERP system. Consequently, cloud-based ERP system is a new integrated approach which can change the functions of business processes and the way users utilise it effectively throughout development. Change management and TOE framework can be a focus for an organisation to implement a cloud-based ERP system successfully.

REFERENCES

[1] Bingi, P., Sharma, M.K. & Godla, J. K. (1999) Critical issues affecting an ERP implementation: Information System Management, 16(3), pp. 7-14.

[2] Jarrar, Y.F., Al-Mudimigh, A., & Zairi, M (2000) ERP implementation critical success factors - The role and impact of business process management: IEEE, 1(1), pp. 122-127.

[3] Low, C. & Chen, Y. (2011) Understanding the determinants of cloud computing adoption: IMDS, 111(7), pp. 1006-1023.

[4] Nah, F. F., Lau, J. L., & Kuang, J. (2001) Critical factors for successful implementation of enterprise system: Business Process Management Journal, 7(3), pp. 285-296.

[5] Ngai, E.W.T., Law, C.C.H., & Wat, F. K. T. (2007) Examining the critical success factors in the adoption of Enterprise Resource Planning: Computer in Industry, 59(6), pp. 1-17.

[6] Rimal, B. P., Jukan, A., Katsaros, D. & Goeleven, Y. (2011) Architectural requirements for cloud computing systems: An enterprise cloud approah: Springer, 9(1), pp. 3-26.

[7] Saini, S. L., Saini, D. K., Yousif, J. H. & Khandage, S. V. (2011) Cloud computing and Enterprise Resource Planning Systems: World Congress on Engineering, I, pp. 681-684.

[8] Schubert, P. & Adisa, F. (2011) Cloud computing for Standard ERP Systems: Reference Framework and Research Agenda: University Koblenz-Landau, 16, pp. 1-17.

[9] Somers, T.M. & Nelson, K. (2001) The Impact of critical success factors across the Stages of Enterprise Resource Planning Implementations: IEEE, 10(1), pp. 1-10

Cloud Computing: Opportunities for Micro Business

Ibrar Ahmed

University of Derby

E-mail: I.Ahmed2@unimail.derby.ac.uk

Abstract—**Cloud computing has developed from being seen as a pronounced idea to becoming one of the leading sectors of the information technology. From this, enterprises are adopting this approach to receive reliable methods and to minimize cost. As micro enterprise decide to approach cloud computing they have to have an understanding on how to use and maintain cloud computing within their organization. "Cloud computing is the evolution of a variety of technologies that have come together to alter an organization's approach to building out an IT infrastructure" [1]. In this article I am going to discuss the opportunities for a micro business when applying cloud in to their organization.**

INTRODUCTION

The first modern approach towards cloud computing was approached by Salesforce.com and Google.com in 1999 [2].Sales force had started and were the leaders of that time for adopting cloud computing for business's on the web. As cloud computing becomes more known major companies started deploy cloud within their organizations. In 2002 Amazon used a cloud application for their storage and performance via Amazon Mechanical Turk. This servives provides; "**On-demand workforce**—Amazon Mechanical Turk provides access to a virtual community of Workers. **Create jobs that Workers perform over the Internet**— Advertise your job to the thousands of Amazon Mechanical TurkWorkers around the worldYou prescribe the job (HIT) that Workers complete using their computer, and pay them for their work. **Test and publish your jobs**—Test your applications in the Amazon Mechanical Turk sandbox Test your jobs in the Amazon Mechanical Turk sandbox and publish the revised jobs to the outside world" [3]. This approach shows how beneficial cloud computing was to Amazon, it saved the company money, time and made the work structure more efficient.

Cloud computing can be seen as a commodity dealer. You buy a product in bulk, break the product down into smaller components and sell or rent at a retail price to individuals. Cloud computing is

Similar to this, methodology suppliers keep their software (product) on the internet. When their software is on the internet it used by clients. This is being paid as the service is being use. You could call this a "pay and go service". So the user only pays for the service he has used. However this is not a definition of cloud computing.

SOFTWARE AS A SERVICE (SAAS)

Software as a service is an application which provides millions of users threw using a browser. "Software as a Service (SaaS) delivers special-purpose software that is remotely accessible by consumers through the Internet with a usage-based pricing model" [4]. SaaS basically is software which is available in the cloud. One of the great aspects of SaaS is that the application does is not limited to any operating system. And as the users you are not bothered about were the software is hosted. The key element is that when using SaaS as a consumer you don't have to install any kind of software which is beneficial for any business because this reduces cost immediately.

An example of SaaS is Gmail. This is just an email application which you use on a browser. Gmail service provides similar applications and structure compared to Outlook or Apple mail. But the key difference is that you do not have a mediator. "Even if your domain does not receive email through Gmail, you can still use Gmail to access your mail" [5]. This one of the key advantages of SaaS, a business can still access the information they require even thon the domain does not allow certain applications. Cloud computing is increasing growing within business. The service that it offers to business and individuals is the opportunity to access their data using a wide range of computer systems.

SaaS has few unique features such as; Availability, Payment plan, Minimal IT demands. **Availability**- to use SaaS on your IT systems it does not require you install any software. The only requirement is that you have a connection to the internet then use SaaS threw a web browser. **Payment Plan**- SaaS does have an installation fee or a complicated set up. As a user you just pay for the service for what you use. You could say it's a pay as you go service. So from a business point of view you only pay for the service you use, and when you have finished using the service you stop paying. **Minimal IT demands**- To use SaaS you don't have to set up any networks or have services within your business. This saves the company time and money.

ADVANTAGES OF CLOUD

Cloud computing has many advantages for a micro business. One of the key advantages of cloud computing is flexibility. This allows business to access their business data in and out of there office, within in office ours or out. As long as they have an internet connection they will be able to access their data. As technologies is adapting day by day business can access their data threw smartphones such as HTC, Blackberry or IPhones. The application is available to staff members of the business. "to take advantage of the best geographic conditions, in order to prevent, within reason, Natural earthquakes and other calamities" [6]. Employees can access the data if they require information; communicate together without physically being there. Information can simultaneously be accessed even though they work force is at different locations.

Another Advantage is it gives an opportunity to small and medium size business to expand their organizations. The businesses only pay for the services they use. In sense it is a pay as you go service. This is how cloud computing saves cost for business. Another aspect of lowering cost is that cloud computing does not require a business to buy and install expensive software. The reason being that cloud computing has the software already installed online for users to access. Another key benefit is that cloud computing offers virtual unlimited storage for business. This reduces cost for business; they do not have to buy as much hard drives and in compression to hard drive cloud computing offers more storage.

Businesses are approaching cloud due to the lower cost of capital for their organization. One of the key advantages of using cloud computing is that allows business to set a certain amount of cost of their own choice. "You can often connect IT costs to revenue instead of treating them as overhead" [7]. Meaning that service they use is only pay as you go again, so it can be seen as a utility like a phone bill or gas.

The table shows the cost comparison of different IT infrastructures. As the table shows that the overall capital cost for cloud computing is cheaper. "cloud computing's usage-based pricing model offers several advantages, including reduced capital expense, a low barrier to entry, and the ability to scale up as demand requires, as well as to support brief surges in capacity"[9]

Table I. Comparing the cost of different IT infrastructures (2008) [8]

Another key advantage for a micro business is that the information is safe on a server. There for less likely to be lost or stolen compared to a hard drive. Business can store copies of data on to their own personal cloud, if a organisation decides not save data on their harddrive.

SECURITY IN CLOUD

	Internal IT	Managed Services	The Cloud
Capital Investment	$40,000	$0	$0
Setup cost	$10,000	£5,000	$1,000
Monthly Service Fees	$0	£4,000	$2,400
Monthly Staff cost	$3,200	£0	$1,000
Net Cost over three years	£149,000	$129,000	$106,000

When a business data is on a server it is understandable to be cautious about using the cloud application. The cloud can be secure or even securer then a data center. When a business is considering using cloud computing it has to have an insight on the issues:

Privacy issues- "cloud computing has significant implications for the privacy of personal information" [10]. This shows that cloud computing has its own security within the cloud.

Data security- Physical access to the server is rare. However this may discomfort users. As they are not aware of the server were all their data is being held. The main issue with this is that anything could happen to the server, it could break down, fire, and maintenance is some of the issues relating to the practical side. These issues may have nothing do with your business however they still could affect a business lost. Other issues could be that your cloud providers declares bankruptcy and the server gets seized in a court settlement; A third party which whom you may not even know sues your server provider, and if your server provider loses they may have to hand over the server. To avoid theses situation the solution is to encrypt sensitive data, and have backups like a second provider. The reason being is that if anything does happen to the server provider you will be able to recover your data.

CONCLUSION

Cloud computing is a growing concept with in the business, government and private sectors. Cloud computing offer substantial advantages such, it will reduce businesses, government or private sectors in its cost. Once a business has started to use cloud, the capital reduces dramatically. However one has to consider, the security issues with in the cloud. Companies may not know where the server is. Is the server being maintained, monitored or is the server in a hazard environment. Even though considering these risks companies still adopt the cloud computing due to the fact that it has huge cost advantages improves the work load, easier access to files and allows small business to work outside their business environment. The paper clearly states that cloud computing is a great opportunity for small business. It gives them and prospect to expand their business and workforce.

References

[1] Reese.G (2009). *Cloud Application Architectures.* Sebastopol: O'Reilly Media.p1.

[2]SalesForce. (2012). A Complete History Of CloudComputing. Available:http://www.salesforce.com/uk/soci alsuccess/cloud-computing/thecomplete-history-of-cloud-computing.jsp.Last accessed 01 Apr 2012.

[3]Amazon Mechanical Turk. (2012). Introduction to Amazon Mechanical Turk. Available: http://docs.amazonwebservices.com/AWSMechTurk/latest/ AWSMechanicalTurkGettingStartedGuide/SvcIntro.html.

[4] Yong Zhao ; Raicu, I. ; Lu, S. (2008). Cloud Computing and Grid Computing 360-Degree Compared. Grid

.

Computing Environments Workshop, 2008. GCE '08. 1 (1), p4.

[5] Reese.G (2009). Cloud Application Architectures. Sebastopol: O'Reilly Media.p2.

[6] Fenu, G.;Surcis, S . (2008). An approach to a Cloud Computing network. Applications of Digital Information and Web Technologies, 2008. . 1 (1), p116

[7] Reese.G (2009). Cloud Application Architectures. Sebastopol: O'Reilly Media.p14

[8] [5] Reese.G (2009). Cloud Application Architectures. Sebastopol: O'Reilly Media.p14

[9] Grossman, R.L. . (2009). The Case for Cloud Computing. IT Professional. 11 (2), 23-27.

[10] Antonopoulos,N; Gillam,L (2010). Cloud Computing Principles, Systems and Applications. London: Springer. p276

Data security issues within cloud computing

Jonathan Bailey

School of Computing and Mathematics

University Of Derby

Derby, United Kingdom

J.Bailey3@derby.ac.uk

Abstract— Within this article will be a discussion of the security threats to data within cloud computing. Throughout the article will be various issues that are common concern amongst organisations that are thinking about migrating to a cloud based system. Each issue will be discussed in detail along with recommendations for counter measures. The article describes the top three data security issues that are currently considered the most important for organizations to consider.

INTRODUCTION

There are various security issues that arise within cloud computing, the main focus of this article is to look into the security risk that involve data. These particular security issues are often a high concern to organisations that will be dealing with potentially important data such as customer information which must be kept private from the public.

The issues being discussed within the article are the most common data security issues within cloud computing these include:

➤ Data loss or destruction

➤ Unauthorised access to data

➤ Availability issues

These security issues are the top three issues that involve data and cloud computing. These security issues are the ones that concern most organisations when thinking about adopting cloud based systems. Each security issue will be analysed along with counter measurement that are currently in place or that could be in place to help prevent these security issues occurring.

These issues are a high concern to organisations as often the data they hold is one of the most important assets that the company may have. The issues all have unique problems and often a solution to those particular issues. This article will study these problems and suggests a solution that would be appropriate to overcome the relevant issues mentioned above.

Figure 1 shows the issues within cloud computing. From this we can tell the top issues regarding cloud computing. From Figure 1 we can see that most organisations are most concerned about security of their data followed by the Figure

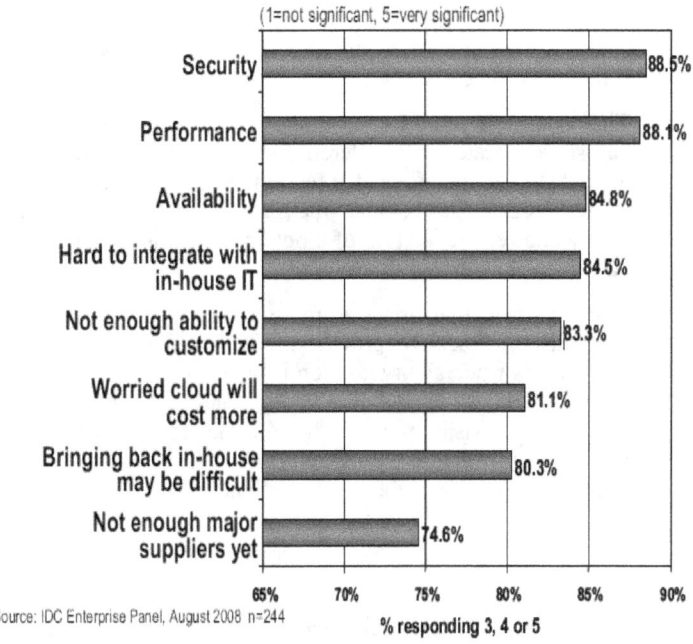

Figure 1.

performance and the final is availability. This helps highlight the areas that can often swing a decisions when potentially adopting cloud computing.

DATA LOSS OR DESTRUCITON

The first issue to be discussed is data loss or the destruction of data. This first issue is in regards to data being lost or destroyed in result of an error or intended sabotage to data.

When migrating data to another system there is always the potentially for data to go astray, this is always a concern for organisations as often the data is valuable and cannot be replaced easily.

When dealing with the administrative privileges and cloud computing this particular user could potentially delete the data which would affect everyone. Along the same lines of this they may purposely delete data that could cause an issue, although this is an unlikely situation. This part of the issues also linked to the second issues of unauthorised access. The second main issue covers any sort of attacks in more detail which could cause harm to the organisation.

The second part of this issue is more about a potential physical destruction. When dealing with cloud computing the data is not stored locally and unless it is backed-up correctly to a secondary site a number of finer issues. For example a fire could cause an immediate issue with the servers that are running the cloud service. These issues could potentially cause the destruction of data. Other issues such as power failures or natural disasters could cause the same problems.

One of the solutions to this is to make sure that the vendor has the required safety precautions. A fire prevention system a uninterruptible power supply (UPS) and a temperature controlled environment. These counter measures will ensure that the premises are not as vulnerable to natural disasters and other rare occurrences.

The counter measure to these main issues is often to have a backup server located in a different location. This ensures that any data that could be affected is securely stored and accessible when required. This counter measure helps improve the reliability and reduce the risk of a potential data loss and even data destruction in extreme cases.

Another issue that arises is more to do when switching between different service providers. The problem is vendor lock ins; this is when an organsation is bounded to their current vendor with a contract. This links to the issues with data loss as if an organsation wishes to switch vendor they may have to pay for this service, if they are unwilling to pay for such a service then the vendor has the right to keep the data.

III. UNAUTHORISED ACCESS TO DATA

The second issue to be discussed is unauthorised access to data. This issue is more to do with a security threat that can occur. Although this security risk is unlikely for the average organsation there is always potential.

The issue has many problems that may occur often these involve attacks from hackers from outside the organsation trying to gain access to data which could potentially be valuable to the organisation. These attacks come in various forms. The most commons forms are:

- Denial of service attacks (DoS)
- Server Spoofing
- IP spoofing
- DNS poising
- Phishing attacks

These types of attacks are the most relevant when dealing with cloud computing as they are either inception of usernames and passwords or to crash the servers or client's personal computers. Each one of these attacks can cause serious harm when dealing with cloud computing. Primarily it is up to the vendor to ensure that their digital security is up to the task of eliminating all types of potentially threats that could occur that may harm the customer's data.

Phishing attacks are amongst the most common although they are more directed at a personal user they can still be a threat to the larger organisation. For example if a phishing e-mail is sent to the IT staff asking them to log into their cloud computing service it may be genuine or this could be a form of attack. Although common sense would think to just ignore this e-mail, however some user may click the log in link and if they fake website is well designed it is an immediate security threat if the user doesn't suspect the attack therefore making the phishing attack a considerable threat to unaware users.

Another form of attack that can be performed is data inception, this is when a hacker rather than going for the servers, they go for the links between the server and user and with this connection they can view what the user is looking at rather than a direct attack. The solution to this is to ensure that there is a secure connection between the users of the service and the servers that are under the vendors control.

Another issue that develops is the physical access to the servers. Although the vendors may have exceptional counter measure to digital attacks they must also make sure that their physical security is complicate with the security needs of the customer. An example of a physical attack is if a person has access to the server farm location and decides to sabotage the server in any form (e.g. remove a memory module or a hard drive (HDD)) then this could cause a ripple effect as data could potentially be lost or corrupted.

Amazon & Amazon web services have put in place physical security layer to help prevent their current system is specially designed to make sure any physical threat cannot be achieved. Below is a statement from a security report of Amazon web services(AWS) of May 2011,

[2]"*Amazon has many years of experience in designing, constructing, and operating large-scale datacenters. This experience has been applied to the AWS platform and infrastructure. AWS datacenters are housed in nondescript facilities. Physical access is strictly controlled both at the perimeter and at building ingress points by professional security staff utilizing video surveillance, intrusion detection systems, and other electronic means. Authorized staff must pass two-factor authentication a minimum of two times to access datacenter floors. All visitors and contractors are required to present identification and are signed in and continually escorted by authorized staff.*"

The above section of the report clearly indicates how organisations that host cloud computing services must be secured to the highest level to ensure that data is secured from any potential physical threat that could occur.

IV. AVAILBAILITY ISSUES

The final issues to be addressed is the availability issues this particular issues can often be classed as a threat to security. When dealing with cloud computing the access to the servers must be constant - any down time could highlight either a system problem or bring up the other issues.Another problem with availability is the security factor. Having an internal server is very useful as it allows constant access to the data even if a internet connection is not present although a physical connection is required to a computer. when you have an internal server you are able to see who has physical access to the server. When dealing with cloud computing this privilege is removed and you are not told who has access, this makes the organisation rely on the organisation delivering the service to make sure either security measures are up to standard to make sure that servers are secure.

The second issues is when the server farm is based in a different country in isolated places. This poses a threat as although it may reduce cooling costs for the service provider if a connection is broken somewhere and there are no redundancies in place to make sure of a stable connection then organisations could be out of contact with their data for extended periods of time. Although these problems may be caused by a natural disaster or server weather connections it's a serious issue that organisation must take into consideration when adopting cloud computing.

This issue can be major for some organisations if no service level agreement is set into place before then organisations may come up short if they are using a cloud based service for a critical business processes. Below is a quote from the organsations Gartner stating the importance of this issue.

[3]*" many cloud-based offerings do not provide service level commitments that are typically needed for critical business processes. Organizations should define service-level requirements for any nontrivial IT workload and demand service-level agreements from the provider"*

V. CONCLUSION

In conclusion these three security threats are what all organisation must consider when dealing with cloud computing weather the organisations is currently using cloud computing or considering migrating to use cloud computing. Each security threat has been described in detail to help give an overview of what needs to be taken into consideration when dealing with cloud computing. Within this conclusion will also be recommendations on how to overcome the security threats that may occur. This will help provide a better insight in how organisations can help defend their clients and equipment against any sort of threat.

The first issue dealing with data loss is a important one for organisation wishing to migrate to the cloud. There will always be risk of certain elements but in more detail the first sub issue dealing with administration privileges would be more to do with when migrating to the cloud as this is when it would be most vulnerable to incorrect information. A simple solution for this is a backup of vital data whether it be on site or off site is always good practice, for vital data multiple backs in varied locations would offer the best solution to avoid any data loss or poential destruction in unforeseen circumstances. The second issue that was discussed about unauthorised access to data is a more constant threat which organisations must consider even when with the cloud as there always a chance that they could

be affect by the mention threats. The main counter measure to this type of threat will often be add layers of security, for example the AWS security measure on physical security. The second security measure is more technical but there are multiple ways to achieve this.

For example firewalls, anti-malware ant-virus software and maybe even virtual private networks may be a solution to stop unauthorised access, the final counter-measure would be always making sure that there is a secure socket layer connection between the client and the data.The final threat discussed is the availability issue; this is often a deciding factor when thinking about migrating to the cloud. Organisations with internal servers normally will have issues but when dealing with cloud computing there is a chance that either a connection is lost to the server due to unforeseen circumstances.This can be seen as a serious threat as organisations can potentially lose temporary access to their customer records which is often vital to organisations. The service-level agreement is a vital way to avoid any availability issues that may occur.

In summary all of these security threat need to be taken into consideration whether or not the organisation has adopted cloud computing. These issues are what can make organisations decided whether or not to migrate to the cloud. The recommendations clearly state way to avoid having any problems occur when dealing with data and security issues.

ACKNOWLEDGMENT

Thank you Dr.Richard Hill for his guidance with this article.

REFERENCES

[1] Dillon, T., "cloud Computing: Issies and Challenges

[2] Amazon, "Amazon Web Services Overview of Security Processes",2011.p.5

[3] Heiser, J. & Nicolett, M., "Assesing the Security Risks of Cloud Computing",2008.p.3

Analysing Whether a Business Should Choose a Hybrid Cloud ERP System Over a Public or Private Cloud System

By Jordan Cordall
School of Computing & Mathematics
University of Derby, UK

Abstract - Cloud computing is the provision of software and applications, data access and the managing and storing of that data over a network. This paper will be looking at businesses that use cloud computing for their enterprise resource planning and whether or not a hybrid system is better than having either a pure public or pure private cloud ERP system.
Keywords – public, private, hybrid, cloud, ERP

BACKGROUND

As more companies are shifting from their standard ERP and legacy systems into Cloud computing and integrating their systems into this it is getting increasingly more important that a business should chose just how their systems are being handled. The business could choose from having a public ERP cloud system, a private ERP cloud system or a hybrid of the two. This article will examine whether or not having a hybrid system is better than having a pure public or private ERP cloud system.

Deciding whether or not a company should be using a public, private or hybrid cloud for its ERP system is an important decision that any company using Cloud technology should consider closely, so that they will be able to get the best from their systems without spending money switching when they find out they made the wrong choice, or having to deal with any problems that could arise from having chosen a pure public Cloud system when they are handling confidential data or having a pure private cloud that needs to be accessed by multiple branches of the company throughout the company.

PUBLIC ERP CLOUDS

A public ERP cloud system is an "off-site" system; this is where the cloud provider has all of the control over the system and is charge. The company then has to pay a subscription fee to the provider for using their services. The service that is available will be a specific programs or applications, these wouldn't be tailor made to suit the users as multiple companies could be using the same kind of system. The cost of the subscription would then depend on the sort of system that the company wants to use and how long they want to use it for.

The positive points of using a public cloud ERP system is that you don't have to spend money on having your own IT department manage and maintain the cloud ERP, and that it is possible to access the system from any computer that is on the network through a web browser. It enables all uses to share storage and servers increasing utilization.

The issue with using a public cloud ERP system is that the business would have to put all of their data, customer details and any trade secrets that they would need in their system, into the hands of the cloud provider. This could cause severe security issues should unauthorised people gain access to all the data due to the providers not having good enough security software in place.

Another issue that could arise is the problem of the provider going into bankruptcy and the company would then find themselves without their ERP system all of a sudden, this could also happen should the providers servers go down. This would mean that the business wouldn't be able to access its important systems and potentially losing business or customers.

PRIVATE ERP CLOUDS

A private ERP cloud system is one that would be classed as an "on-site" system, this is where the servers and system are all located on the premises of the business. By having the system this close it means that it is the responsibility of the business to maintain and mange it. Because of this the business wouldn't have to pay out subscription fees to providers to host their ERP system, however it does mean that the IT department would have to be trained to deal with the system and know how to run it.

Having a private ERP cloud system means that the business has more control and direction over the system, they can customize the system to exactly how they want it, they can also implement and update the security of the system to their own standards to make sure that nothing happens to it.

Because the system is private, not everyone on the network would be able to just gain access to the ERP system and be able to see all of the information that is stored there, users would be given access rights to make sure the data is kept secure.

The negative points of using a private cloud ERP system is that the business doesn't gain the economic benefits of only having to hire the system our from a provider, but this is compensated by the extra security and privacy for the data that is being stored.

HYBRID ERP CLOUDS

The hybrid ERP cloud system is a mixture of both the public and the private cloud systems, in this approach the company has a private cloud to keep all of the sensitive and confidential data secure and in their control so that it cannot be accessed by unauthorised people, all other data can then be stored on the public cloud.

Because of the way that this set up works the business gains the benefit of the security from the private cloud system that they would keep onsite while all publicly accessible data is kept off site by the provider, because of this, if there was an attack on the providers servers then any data that could be taken would be of lower risk than that of customer names and address that would still be on the company premises.

Should the company have to a surge of information that has to be uploaded and dealt with all at the same time then it will be possible to offload some of this onto the public section of the system to help free up internal resources.

Some of the problems with a hybrid ERP cloud system is that it doesn't fully take advantage of either public or private cloud types so it does not gain all the benefits of both. This type of system also means that the business is having to pay out a monthly or yearly subscription to the service provider as well as paying for the staff to maintain and run the private system.

CONCLUSIONS

In conclusion it would be better for a company to have a hybrid system for their ERP Cloud system rather than a public or private ERP cloud system, the hybrid system would be better suited to the larger businesses that would be able to afford to implement and maintain both the public and private sectors of the hybrid system. However if a company wasn't able to afford the cost of running a hybrid cloud then the next best choice would be the private cloud system as it gives greater security than the public system..

REFERENCES

Muzafar Ahmad Bhat et al, *"Cloud Computing: A solution to Information Support Systems (ISS)"*, International Journal of Computer Applications (0975 – 8887) Volume 11 – No.5 December 2010.
URL:
http://www.ijcaonline.org/volume11/number5/pxc3872118.pdf

Maneesha Sharma et al, *"Cloud Computing: Different Approach & Security Challenge"*, International Journal of Soft Computing and Engineering (IJSCE), ISSN: 2231-2307, Volume-2, Issue-1, March 2012.
URL:
http://www.ijsce.org/attachments/File/v2i1/A0469022112.pdf

Bhaskar Prasad Rimal et al, *"Architectural requirements for cloud computing systems: an enterprise cloud approach"*, J Grid Computing (2011) 9:3-26.
URL:
http://www.springerlink.com/content/q08q5140010014k8/fulltext.pdf

S L Saini et al, *"Cloud Computing and Enterprise Resource Planning Systems"*, Proceedings of the World Congress on Engineering 2011 Vol I WCE 2011, July 6 - 8, 2011, London, U.K.

URL:
http://www.iaeng.org/publication/WCE2011/WCE2011_pp681-684.pdf

Cautious Cloud Computing

Security Solutions For Cloud Computing

Joe Lamb
University of Derby
Mansfield, England
100224671@unimail.derby.ac.uk

Abstract— **The following article will be looking at methods to prevent unauthorized access to a company's database within cloud computing discovering what the best solution is for a company who needs to implement a security system, but maybe does not have the knowhow to do so.**

Keywords-component; Cloud Computing; Security; Data loss; Implement.

INTRODUCTION

Offering a next generation, high scalability, money saving package there is no wonder organizations are jumping on the bandwagon of cloud computing. Cloud computing is a system whereby users can upload and pull data from at anytime from anywhere. Gartner suggests the word "cloud" possibly comes from the fact something big and accessible but externally opaque. [1]

The first vision of cloud computing can be traced back as far as the sixties by J.C.R Licklider who was responsible for the development of ARPANET (Advanced Research Projects Agency Network) had the visualization of fully working "Intergalactic computer network". Licklider's vision was for everyone on the globe to be interconnected and be able to access data from anywhere [2] 50 years later we can see Licklder's dream emerged as an essential technology. A recent survey on revenue from Gartner suggested the cloud market will be worth USD 58.6B in 2009, USD 68B in 2010 and will reach USD 148B by 2014. [1]

Data stored in the cloud is becoming increasingly sensitive. Organizations have the added pressure of knowing if their company or clients details get breached the consequences can be terminal. Not many clients want to use a company where by their personal details will or have gone missing in the past.

SECURITY

A. Introduction to security

With data on the cloud being extremely valuable security is taken very seriously. If security gets breached within some organizations causing them to close their site for a period of time, this can lose them millions of pounds as proven by Amazon e.g. For every minute Amazon.com is down they lose $17,050. This is why Amazon invests so much in contingency plans every year.

Security is one of the main issues to consider whilst implementing and maintaining the system. This maybe because the company has the responsibility to keep personal details of others secure such as bank details, addresses, phone numbers etc.

B. Data Loss

An issue with cloud computing security is that investigating illegal action maybe in some cases impossible. Cloud services are difficult to investigate, because logging and data for multiple customers may be co-located and may also be spread across an ever-changing set of hosts and data centres. [2]

A concerning factor of cloud computing is the fact that the company who is monitoring the customers data, do not know where the data is held. This can lead to leaked information from the company that owns the servers. Someone could also potentially break through the security in order to retrieve data from a company's database. Rakshit says even if we don't know where your data is, a cloud provider should tell us what will happen to our data and service in case of a disaster[2]

Shucheng Yu believes Communication channel between the data owner/users and Cloud Servers are assumed to be secured under existing security protocols such as SSL. [3]

SSL stands for Secure Socket Layer and was developed to transfer private documents via the internet. SSL uses two keys to encrypt data to ensure its security.

The University of South Africa, Pretoria think The biggest challenge in implementing successful Cloud Computing technologies is managing the security [security In cloud computing]

VI. PRECAUTIONS

A. Considering A Third Party

The easiest way to implement security in to an organization is to hand it over to a third party. In the article how secure is your network Greg Shipley talks about passing the buck and says outsourcing is quite tempting from the midlevel management perspective. Outsource a heated area to the purported experts and let them deal with the problems. If anything goes wrong, hey, that's not your fault--it was outsourced, right? Unfortunately, it's not always this simple. Security -outsourcing firms can do a few things quite well. [4]

This could also suggest that your company could lose control by outsourcing your security work to another company could also be adding to the problem as there is another team of people could have access to your organizations database. Gartner thinks if a company is considering using a third party service to protect their data then it needs to consider the following risks.

• Assess the security, privacy and regulatory compliance risks

• Identify use cases that are inappropriate for this service delivery method, based on risk
  level and current controls

• Identify use cases that pose an acceptable level of risk for the service delivery method

• Choose and implement compensating controls before going fully operational [1]

B. Preventing Data Loss

Prevention of data loss can be as simple as contracting the right vendor. An organization should not contract a vendor that refuse to provide detailed information on its security and should continually monitor, update and maintain their security to keep the data safe.

Make sure the employees who have access to the data on the server can be trusted as they could be making unauthorized use of the external service. Gartnet says they could create unrecognized information-related risks [1]

Christopher leidigh thinks that the following security measures are essential in any enterprise network security policy:

Essential to security
Firewalls at all public-private network transit points
Version controlled and centrally deployed firewall rule sets
External resources placed in dual firewall, DMZ protected networks
All network hosts lock down unneeded network ports, turn off unneeded services
All network hosts include centrally managed anti-virus software
All network hosts utilize central security updates
Secure central authentication such as Radius, Windows/Kerberos/Active Directory
Centrally managed user management with password policy (i.e. must change every three months and must be "secure password"
Proactive network scanning for new hosts, out of date systems
Network monitoring for suspicious behaviour
Incident response mechanisms (policies, manual, automated, etc.)

[5]

HOW DATA IS LOST

So many procedures are put in place in order to keep the customers data secure and sometimes it still leaks out or somebody breaches the security. Encryption accidents are one of the main reasons a company loses a customer's data. This makes the data totally unusable [1]

HOW DO WE EVALUATE RISK

In order to prevent security breaches, how do we evaluate security risks in times that we need to? Gartner reckons three questions need to be asked to evaluate the security and continuity risks associated with a cloud offering.

Risks	Solutions
How qualified are the policymakers, architects, coders and operators to understand and reduce the risks of their offering?	Accept whatever assurances the service provider offers.
What risk control processes and technical mechanisms are used?	Evaluate the service provider in person.
What level of testing has been done to verify that the service and control processes are functioning as designed and to identify unanticipated vulnerabilities?	Use a neutral third party to perform a security assessment.

[1]

The most practical way to evaluate the risks associated with using a service in the clout is to get a third party to do it as many organizations have no ability in house to adequately assess the security of a sophisticated offering [1].

CONCLUSION

Security is something that should be taken seriously within every company especially the ones holding sensitive data

such as banks and shopping websites. If places like this lose information their business will lose a lot of custom and potentially end.

The best solution appears to be handing over the security to a third party as many businesses do not have the knowledge and experience to implement a sophisticated system and keep it updated. A third party company will specialize in keeping the data within a system secure and will have the experience and know how to do this. They will also have the latest ways to prevent hackers from entering the system.

The security can make or break a company as if the system has been hacked into once, customers will probably believe it can happen again no matter what procedures have been put in place leaving the company with a depleted customer base. A perfect example happened at the bank of Santander where information got leaked. Now the bank are struggling as they lost a lack of trust from its user base and are fighting to stay afloat in today's competitive market.

REFRENCES

[1] Jay Heiser and Mark Nicolett, "Assessing the Security Risks of Cloud Computing," p. 6, June 2008.

[2] Atanu Rakshit and Paturi Ramakrishna, "Cloud Security Issues," p. 4, 2009.

[3] Shucheng Yu, "Achieving Secure, Scalable, and Fine-grained Data," pp. 2-3, 2010.

[4] Greg Shipley, "Outscourcing Security: Pass the Buck," *How Secure is your Network*, p. 8, 2000.

[5] Christopher Leidigh, "Fundamental Principals of Network Security," p. 14, 2005.

Cloud Migration: How to Migrate Enterprise IT Systems to IaaS

Cost modelling and benefits and risk assessment

Author: Krzysztof Ciszak

University of Derby, United Kingdom

Chris.ciszak@gmail.com

Abstract— **Cloud computing is an emerging technology and it looks initially attractive for many companies because it offers many benefits such cost savings and reduced IT workload. But why aren't companies using it more. This article answers how to do cost estimation and risk assessments before companies switch their services and infrastructure to cloud based environment.**

Keywords-component; cloud computing; legacy systems; service selection; software migration; cost modelling, risk assessment

INTRODUCTION

Cloud computing is one of the newest emerging technologies and has made a significant impact on TI industry. It is suitable for creating and maintaining flexible and scalable systems. An increasing number of companies are expected to change their infrastructure and make use of cloud business solutions. However most of companies have legacy elements not designed for cloud use and the most challenging part is to select cloud software solutions and migration of those legacy applications to the cloud efficiently. There are advantages and disadvantages of cloud computing so companies should consider if migrating is a good move. Sometimes only a few parts of the system could be migrated and companies still should benefit from cloud features. Currently there are applications which could help with system migration but unfortunately they have some limitations such as listed below:

- Require legacy application's source code

- Cannot customize the migrated application to meet enterprises' updating requirement.

- Cannot make further mash-up application

- The migration workload is huge

Many enterprise are still not sure what factors should be considered before the migration and how Enterprises should plan migration of their legacy infrastructure to the cloud. If a company wants to switch one or all of their information technology to the cloud they need to understand the costs and risks associated with cloud migration. Also it is very important to understand how it is going to affect their business processes. Section II in this paper will analyze how costs estimation should be prepared and compared with different options. Benefits and risk assessment are another very important factors in any project including cloud migration and it is described in section III of this paper.

DECISION SUPPORT TOOLS

Cloud computing offers many benefits to all companies which could possibly save them lots of money. Unfortunately decision to migrate existing systems to public IaaS clouds is not that straightforward. Enterprises need to evaluate the benefits, risks and costs of using cloud solutions and to do that they need to consider a few different vendors to decide which one will be the best option. Companies may have heard about benefits of cloud computing and different vendors but before they migrate they need to think if the conditions are right for them. To find out when it is the right time to migrate to the cloud they need to evaluate costs and benefits and risk assessments. To deal with it a special software has been created called Cloud Deployment Toolkit which can be installed on Eclipse IDE – a very popular application for developers.

COST MODELLING

Clearly, the most important question is how much the company could save and what are the potential business benefits the company may receive from the cloud. If the benefits of the cloud and the cost of switching is satisfactory to the company they may decide to migrate. Before deciding to migrate Enterprise IT Systems to Cloud there are several types of costs which need to be considered such as: software licenses, IT infrastructure, staff costs, data centre equipment, systems engineering, software changes and so on. In fact Amazon provides spreadsheets for cost comparison which help calculate most of these costs. However, utility billing system in cloud computing makes it more difficult to accurately predict costs with spreadsheets of using IaaS clouds solutions. This doubt refers to:

1. The actual resources consumed by a system, which are determined by its load;
2. The deployment options used by a system, which can affect its costs as things like data transfer are more expensive between clouds compared to data transfer within clouds;
3. Cloud providers' prices, which can change at short notice.

To help companies with the above difficulties a cost modeling tool has been developed which simplifies cost calculations for the deployment of a planned IT system across different clouds. It is a part of Cloud Deployment

Toolkit(CDTK). The CDTK is a set of tools which allows developers to create and build models of their production environment on cloud infrastructure. Using this software companies can calculate a baseline usage for each resource. Project management and software cost estimation techniques are also a part of cost modeling and can increase cost of cloud migration. The cost modeling tool can be used by IT architect to model the company's infrastructure. The tool provides prices from many cloud vendors and produces reports showing how the cost will change over time. UML diagrams are used to show the model of existing infrastructure. Cloud Deployment Toolkit(CDTK) is a separate module which can be installed on the Eclipse IDE and it extends the toolkits diagrams to include:

- Virtual Machine- specifies operation system and server information.

- Virtual Storage - includes storage size, type(e.g. AWS.EBS or AWS.S3), and the number of requests per month.

- Application - specifies applications that are installed on virtual machines.

- Data - specifies applications data that is stored on virtual storage.

- Database - includes databases such as Amazon's Relational Database Service or Microsoft's SQL Azure

- Remote node - represents nodes which are not included on the cloud such as desktop PC's and in-house servers

- Communication Path - represents data flow between any nodes.

- Deployment - shows us the deployment of applications onto virtual machines, or data onto virtual storage.

Created model is used to compare prices with different cloud providers for each node. This gives companies flexibility to ensure they will choose the cheapest solutions for their businesses. The tool is very easy to use because of its drag and drop graphic user interface. Computations include: virtual machines and storage running time and the amount of data requests for storage and any data in and out any nodes.

The tool allows enterprises to find out how much each resource is going to cost the company over time. Resources might be used temporarily or permanently and the application is able to work it in. The cloud has many benefits for all businesses. One of them is its flexibility which lets companies to pay for as much resource as they can use. The tool use a special pattern which helps to count the cost and it looks as follows:

[temp/perm]: every [months] on [days][variation][number]

The following values can be used:

Months	Days	Variations	Numbers
month, jan-dec;	[empty], everyday, weekdays, weekends, 01-31, mon-sun;	+, -, *, /, ^;	float, integer;

For example, if a company requires 80GB of storage, and every month it increases by 5GB, the required storage is halved during weekends between June and August; and it is doubled every December between 25th and 30th. The patter for this scenario would look as follows:

Baseline: 80, Patterns:
perm: every month +5,
temp: every jun-aug on weekends /2,
temp: every dec on 25-30 * 2

Once a cloud deployment and baseline patterns have been created, users need to set a start and end date and the tool will simulate the cost of running such a cloud infrastructure. The program produces graphs which are easy for users to see which options are the best for their requirements. Graphs represent resource' behavior between the start and end dates. Baseline usage is multiplied by the cost of that resource for the specified cloud provider. There are more than 600 providers' prices included in XML file where even more can be added easily. Some of the providers are AWS, GoGrid, FlexiScale, MS Azure, Rackspace and ReliaCloud. Generated report includes embedded graphs, tables and is adapted to review even large systems models thank zoomable option. All data can be downloaded as a CSV file which is opened by Excel. The software can create models for different groups and estimate costs separately. A group can be a department in a company, an organization or just some part of a system. Thank that architects can estimation different option for particular parts of the system and choose the cheapest.

BENEFITS AND RISK ASSESMENT

There are still not many enterprises deciding to move to the cloud because its complicated a process for more advanced systems. Costs savings are one of the most important benefits but before enterprise decide to migrate to the cloud several other factors need to be examined. How it is going to affect client relationships, flexibility, public image, business continuity and adaptation. Because of so many issues related to cloud migration, a benefits and risk assessment tool has been developed and it is a part of the CDTK.

According to [1] more than 50 academic papers were investigated to find out more about benefits and risks during cloud migration. They were categorized as technical, legal, security, financial and organizational. A few examples can be seen in Table 1(full lists are available on ShopForCloud.com).

This spreadsheet is a great starting point because it can help evaluate risk assessment describing the potential danger and consequences. Architects can go through the list and rate each risk as unimportant, little important, moderately important, important, or very important from their perspective.

According to Institute of Information Security Professionals workshop [3] many companies do not have the right understanding of their security management lifecycle, and many of these companies will face similar issues when they migrate to the cloud. When a company move their internal IT environment to the cloud which relies on a 3rd party suppliers, it will change the way how they manage security and risk. It is very important that companies review the list of potential risks and benefits before deciding if migrating to the cloud is the best option. Only this way they can make sure that the risk will be as low as possible.

TABLE 1. EXAMPLES OF RISKS OF USING PUBLIC IAAS CLOUDS, THE FULL LIST IS AVAILABLE FROM SHOPFORCLOUD.COM

ID	Risk	Mitigation approaches & potential indicators
R1	**Organizational:** Loss of governance and control over resources (both physical control and managerial), might lead to unclear roles and responsibilities, e.g. users can purchase computing resources using their credit cards without explicit approval from central IT.	Clarify roles and responsibilities before cloud adoption.
R26	**Technical:** Major service interruption resulting in extensive outages and unavailability of services or loss of data.	Use multiple cloud providers, monitor applications from outside the cloud. Replicating the system across multiple clouds has associated costs and technical challenges.
R31	**Technical:** Interoperability issues between clouds as there are incompatibilities between cloud providers' platforms.	Use cloud middleware (e.g. RightScale) to ease interoperability issues.
R36	**Financial:** Increased costs due to complex integrations. Inability to reduce costs due to unrealizable reductions in sys-support staff.	Investigate system integration issues upfront, avoid migrating highly interconnected systems initially

CASE STUDY

Migration of Enterprise IT system to Cloud requires knowledge about many factors such as cost estimations and benefits and risk assessments. There is still lack of academic work which examines aspects of cloud migration. A great example of migrating large enterprise in oil industry to the IaaS can be found here [4]. However the main case study in this paper will be about CiteSeer [1] because it used the CDTK described in previous sections.

A. Digital Library and Search Engine

CiteSeer is a well known digital library and search engine which uses highly technical system maintained by a small team. Similarly to IEEE explore, CiteSeer stores academic papers and enables users to search and view them online. The system is built in service-oriented architecture with many different components such as: the main interface where users connects with the system, a maintenance service, document crawling, ingestion and data backup. The system is deployed on 15 servers and has around 2 million hits per day with over 1.5 million documents which is around 2TB of data.

1) Cost Modelling

The cost was estimated using the CDTK based on historical analysis many elastic patterns were created using 3 different vendors. Due to increasing number of visitors and articles CiteSeer required 15GB increase in data every month. The table below represents costs estimation for CiteSeer.

TABLE 2. COST DIFFERENCE[1]

Cost($)	*AWS US-East*	*FlexiScale*	*Rackspace*
1st Month	18 900	5 060	6 550
Monthly avg	1,916	5 151	6 732
Total 3 years	85 950	185 345	242 170
Difference with AWS		2x	3x

As we can see from the table above it is very important to estimate costs over a long period avoiding any disappointments. Potentially the most expensive AWS is the cheapest option over 3 year and more.

2) Risk Assessments

Benefits and risk assessments spreadsheet was used to see potential benefits and issues. 7 benefits and 13 risks were marked as important.

SUMMARY

In this paper cost modeling and benefits and risk assessment were critically evaluated and explained how to prepare before we move to the cloud. Cloud migration is a very difficult process and special tools might help make a decision if a particular enterprise should migrate to cloud. Cloud Adoption Toolkit supports cloud adoption decisions in Enterprise and both tools described above are parts of it. The cost modeling tools allows IT architects to model their data, applications and infrastructure requirements and costs. What is more the benefits and risks assessment tool provide information about security, organizational, legal, technical and financial benefits and risks of using IaaS clouds. Although cloud computing brings many benefits to organizational structure, there are still not many Enterprises which migrate to cloud. Enterprises may not decide to migration to the cloud if they existing systems performance meets their requirements. However, additions to existing systems might be a great option for cloud computing as it is improbable that they will suffer from migration issues.

REFERENCES

[1] Khajeh-Hosseini, A.; Sommerville, I.; Bogaerts, J.; Teregowda, P.; , "Decision Support Tools for Cloud Migration in the Enterprise," *Cloud Computing (CLOUD), 2011 IEEE International Conference on* , vol., no., pp.541-548, 4-9 July 2011 doi: 10.1109/CLOUD.2011.59

[2] Xin Meng; Jingwei Shi; Xiaowei Liu; Huifeng Liu; Lian Wang; , "Legacy Application Migration to Cloud," *Cloud Computing (CLOUD), 2011 IEEE International Conference on* , vol., no., pp.750-751, 4-9 July 2011 doi: 10.1109/CLOUD.2011.56

[3] Yam, C.-Y.; Baldwin, A.; Shiu, S.; Ioannidis, C.; , "Migration to Cloud as Real Option: Investment Decision under Uncertainty," *Trust, Security and Privacy in Computing and Communications (TrustCom), 2011 IEEE 10th International Conference on* , vol., no., pp.940-949, 16-18 Nov. 2011 doi: 10.1109/TrustCom.2011.130

[4] Khajeh-Hosseini, A.; Greenwood, D.; Sommerville, I.; , "Cloud Migration: A Case Study of Migrating an Enterprise IT System to IaaS," *Cloud Computing (CLOUD), 2010 IEEE 3rd International*

Conference on, vol., no., pp.450-457, 5-10 July 2010
doi: 10.1109/CLOUD.2010.37

[5] Mastroeni, L.; Naldi, M.; , "Long-range Evaluation of Risk in the Migration to Cloud Storage," *Commerce and Enterprise Computing*

(CEC), 2011 IEEE 13th Conference on , vol., no., pp.260-266, 5-7 Sept. 2011
doi: 10.1109/CEC.2011.47

Cloud Computing: The New Change Management

Katie Elizabeth Manning

School of Computing and Mathematics

University of Derby, UK

100081952@unimail.derby.ac.uk

Abstract— **Traditional Enterprise Resource Planning (ERP) systems are implemented on a company's on premise server and controlled by the company under their supervision, where cloud based ERP systems are hosted, supported and maintained fully by the external vendor; therefore taking away a lot of the technical aspects in which on premise staff, would usually deal with during and after the implementation of the ERP system.**

This paper aims to discuss how cloud computing is becoming the new change management by removing those technological aspects and focusing more on the business processes.

Keywords; change management; cloud computing; enterprise resource planning; on-premise ERP; organisational change.

BACKGROUND

A. What is change management?

Change management is a planned approach towards a change within an organisation. It has been identified that change management is one of the most critical success factors within implementing an ERP system [1] and more often, ERP implementation projects fail due to the lack of change management. The implementation of an ERP system may require re-engineering of business processes and/or the development of new processes in order to support the business goals [2]. Therefore it is critical that a change management process is in place, in order to prepare and ensure that a smooth transition takes place.

B. Change management case study: University of Derby staff intranet

When the University of Derby introduced plans to implement a new staff intranet, many staff members were resistant, as it was an entirely new process in which they would need to get used to. During the implementation stage of the project, training was provided for only select members of each department, which eventually at a later date would be rolled out to other members in the departments. In addition, there was only one member of staff from IT services assigned to each department in order to provide help in setting up their departments' site, however due to the fact there was not enough IT service staff to cover all of the departments, they had to be shared out and each member of staff from IT services had to cover multiple departments. Staff members soon became very negative of the new system due to: long training sessions that only provided introductory level instructions, the software was extremely difficult to use and departments had to wait long

periods of time to request for help in setting up new sites, hence the reason why many department intranet sites stayed dormant during and after the implementation of the new intranet system. Eventually all of the sites were successfully created, however many staff members did not want to update them regularly due to the trouble and difficulty that they would face when using the system. This case study illustrates the consequences of what happens when an efficient change management process has not been implemented. It also demonstrates how the difficulty of an on-premise ERP system can cause low morale for members of staff, which in time could be catastrophic for a company. Future developments may also be problematic as members of staff will be reluctant to change, if a previous change in the company has not ran smoothly or been successful.

C. The change curve

Illustrated in fig. 1 is Menninger's morale curve [3]; showing the state of a person's morale when a change takes place. The graph demonstrates four states of change in which a person will go through, these are: arrival, engagement, acceptance and re-entry. As illustrated in the graph, levels of morale will be significantly higher when the change approaches; staff may be motivated and enthusiastic about the change. However, when the change begins to take place, morale drops severely; staff members may show signs of frustration and fear. The levels then begin to rise slightly when the change has eventually begun to be accepted, and lastly the level of morale equals out when the change has been re-evaluated or finally accepted.

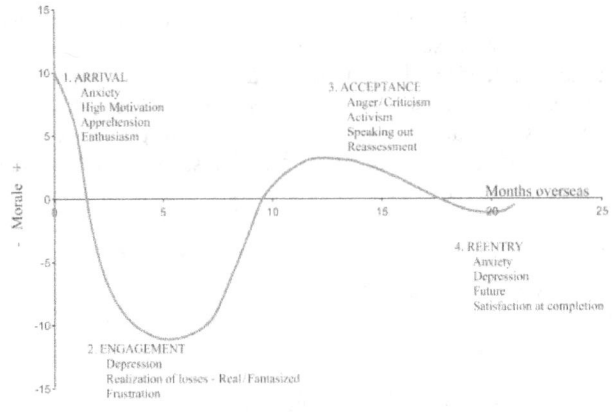

Figure 1. Menninger's Morale Curve

D. What is cloud computing?

Cloud computing is a delivery model; the technology and the concept of storing content online already existed before the term "cloud computing" arose. Cloud computing is a technical term for migrating services, data and software onto a remote server; providing computing as an online service, rather than a product, thus allowing users to access their content with just a computer and an internet connection. An example of a cloud service is iCloud; all content such as photos, music, contacts, emails and any other content that is stored on the apple device, is automatically synchronized to the iCloud. This content can then be shared to other apple devices that are owned.

E. Service computing

Service computing is a way of taking the system requirements of a business and providing them as a service on a cloud network. The business would not be responsible for the infrastructure or the platform of the system, the external vendor would take on this responsibility; meaning the clients can specify what their system needs are, in a non-technical approach, without having to know any of the back-end technical aspects, such as databases and servers. Service computing could potentially prove more successful with the change management process. Companies will be outsourcing and paying a vendor to provide computing as a service and taking on the full technical responsibilities of the project, meaning that:

- On-premise staff will no longer have to change their roles/responsibilities to accommodate for the ERP implementation.

- IT staff can proceed with normal roles such as PC maintenance and other IT projects.

- Staff can shift their focus from IT to business

- Morale will remain calm, proactive and staff will be less likely to resist the change if they know they won't be affected dramatically by the new change.

ADOPTING CLOUD

A. Key issues about adopting cloud

The main key issue for adopting a cloud based service is business processes. It is fundamental that the business processes, needs and requirements are identified before making the decision to deploy a cloud based ERP system. There needs to be a sound understanding of how current processes will be migrated onto the cloud system and also how these changes will be managed.

B. Key issues about adopting any new technology

As with any new technology there are elements that should be taken into consideration before making any decisions, some of these might be:

- Is the technology going to provide value to the company?
- How much of an impact will it have on staff?

- How much will it cost?
- Is it easy to use, implement and train employees on?
- Will it integrate with existing systems, including those that are not cloud based?
- Are there enough internal resources to cope with implementation and the management of the new system?

C. What is different about cloud adoption?

In contrast to on premise ERP systems, the initial cost of a cloud based ERP system is much lower because the implementation only involves the specifically required software; the user can then access the software through an internet connection, whereas on premise ERP systems usually consists of large-scale implementations that run for long periods of time. The infrastructure of an ERP system is fairly expensive. Organisations can embrace and implement ERP systems that are based on the cloud due to how economical they are in cost [4].

The cloud ERP provider will host and maintain the entire infrastructure for the organisation and ensure that the system is always running and that data is secure; meaning IT resources can focus on helping the organisation grow more effectively rather than spending their time maintaining the on premise ERP system. Upgrades and enhancements will also be left to the provider with no additional investment. Cloud ERP systems often deliver better performance than on premise systems as the architecture of cloud software is designed for maximum network performance. If an organisation recognises the business processes, then adopting a cloud based ERP system can make the change management process easier. Smaller organisations tend to understand their business processes better so if a higher education institution were to adopt a cloud based ERP system; it would be vital for them to firstly understand the processes in order to adopt an efficient change management process that will satisfy the needs and requirements, in order for the business to run efficiently.

CLOUD BASED ERP SYSTEMS

A. Traditional ERP flowchart Vs. Cloud based ERP

Four factors have been identified by [4] that exist within a traditional ERP system implementation flowchart, these are:

- Hire consultants to select software

- Install ERP system

- Configure system

- Maintenance of the system.

In comparison to the cloud based ERP flow chart that [4] has also provided, none of these factors would be necessary if a company was to deploy a cloud based ERP system, thus removing what would appear to be, the most difficult stages of an ERP implementation; making it a very beneficial for a company by allowing them to focus all efforts on driving the business forward.

B. Change management barriers that exist with on-premise ERP systems

Below are some characteristics that have been identified by [5] as critical failure factors for ERP implementation, these factors can make managing the change within an organisation difficult. Also included with each point below is an explanation of, if and how these will be evident with a cloud based ERP system:

- Inadequate training – training would still be required with a cloud based ERP system

- Poor IT infrastructure – the cloud vendor would be responsible for this

- Resistance to change by staff – may still be resistance but with the technological aspects removed, the business can focus on the staff and easing them into the new ERP processes.

- Poor quality of business process re-engineering – this will be made easier with the cloud based ERP system

- Poor quality of testing – cloud vendor would be responsible for this

- Tight project schedule – cloud based ERP systems typically involve quick implementations, meaning tight schedules can be achievable.

C. Comparison of responsibilities

Table 1 shows a comparison between the key responsibilities for adopting either an on-premise ERP system or a cloud based system:

TABLE I.

Responsibility	On-premise staff	Cloud based ERP vendor
Designing the IT infrastructure	✓	✓
Testing	✓	✓
Project Team	✓	N/A
Maintenance	✓	✓
Upgrades	✓	✓
Fixing issues	✓	✓
Project consultant	✓	✓
System Integrators	✓	✓

The table clearly illustrates that if an on-premise ERP system is to be implemented then responsibilities lie solely within the business; meaning high costs, time and efforts being put forward to implement the system. On the other hand, a cloud based ERP system vendor can take all of the hassle and responsibility away from an on-premise ERP implementation and offer a full, cost effective monthly service. A number of benefits have been listed by [6] in which cloud computing can offer to a business, some of which are: scalability, agility, better IT resource management, rapid developments and change management, improved security and better performance and as [7] states, cloud computing allows smaller organisations the opportunity to have access to a larger IT infrastructure that would typically not be available.

CONCLUSION

There is clear evidence relating to how difficult it is to carry out an affective change management process with on-premise ERP systems and many projects fail due to the fact that technology is always the core focus, meaning the people who would essentially be dealing with the change, are forgotten. In order for a change within an organisation to be successful, it is critical to focus on the people first. An external vendor can offer an easier, more stable solution for a business and take full responsibility of the support of the cloud based ERP system, allowing an organisation to spend more time to focus on the business as appose to spending large amounts of time and resources focusing on the technology. Furthermore, cloud computing is transforming the change management process by removing the difficult technological aspects that would usually be involved in an on-premise ERP system implementation and allowing a business to focus on the people and the business processes, making cloud computing a vital part in the future success of a business and also creating an easier, successful change management process.

REFERENCES

[1] ALdayel, A. I., ALdayel, M. S., & Al-Mudimigh, A. (2011, October). The Critical Success Factors of ERP implementation in Higher Education in Saudi Arabia: A Case Study. Journal of Information Technology and Economic Development, 2(2), 1-16.

[2] Rabaa'i, A. A. (2009). Identifying critical success factors of ERP systems at the higher education sector. ISIICT 2009: Third International Symposium on Innovation in Information & Communication Technology, (pp. 1-15). Amman.

[3] Tippett, D. D., & Elrod, D. P. (2002). The "death valley" of change. Journal of Organizational Change Management, 15(3), 273-291.

[4] Motalab, M. B., & Shohag, S. A. (2011, August). Cloud Computing and the Business Consequences of ERP Use. International Journal of Computer Applications (0975 - 8887), 28(8), 31-37.

[5] Wong, A., Scarbrough, H., Davison, R., & Chau, P. Y. (2005). Critical Failure Factors in ERP Implementation. 9th Pacific Asia Conference on Information Systems (PACIS 2005), (pp. 492-505). Bangkok.

[6] Carroll, M., & Kotze, P. (2011). Secure Cloud Computing: Benefits, Risks and Controls. Information Security South Affrica (ISSA), (pp. 1-9). Pretoria.

[7] Mahmood, Z. (2011). Cloud Computing: Characteristics and Deployment Approaches. 11th IEEE International Conference on Computer and Information Technology, (pp. 121-126).

Approaches in managing user profiles in cloud based ERP systems

Kamil Stosik
University of Derby
School of computing and mathematics, Derby
k.stosik1@unimail.derby.ac.uk

Abstract: In an ERP cloud based system user profiles are essential to provide security. The article describes the Internet based user access, user groups maintained in the system and authorization levels. Then, it takes a deeper look at management of user profiles along with presentation of necessary tools, to eventually summarize and answer the question of whether user profiling is beneficial for the system or rather is an unnecessary complication for the users.

Keywords: ERP, system, users, user profiles, cloud, security, management

INTRODUCTION

Every ERP system has a demand for a high security level. Especially, when looking at the newest approaches of ERPs where most of them are moving to the cloud based storage systems. With Internet access, systems are exposed to more threats than ever before which leads to the requirement of more secure systems and solutions. One of the protections is user profiling. It is a basic protection that creates user in the system, tracks their moves and allows access to various parts of the system. End-user only sees his login page and basically that part is over for him. Real challenge begins when one takes a deeper look into the system and tries to determinate how these users are categorized, assigned to different groups and what permissions do they have in the system. Another significant part of this protection is tools that help to create proper groups and facilitate managing and maintaining them. Finally, balance between security and ease of use are at stake when creating a proper authorizations system which may affect users accessing different data and different parts of the system, therefore there should be a properly determined strategy of data flow and data access which minimize the risk of inaccessible content for the users and also protects the content that should only be visible to selected group of users.

USER PROFILES IN CLOUD ERP SYSTEM

A. User profiling

User profiling is an important part of the systems managed automatically by algorithms and scripts, which implement functions that are triggered in case of an event that occurred dynamically by a user action and its level access in the system in order to exchange data. After the connection is initialized, it is only valid until the data exchange session does not expire. Scripts are based on pre-written scenarios. Level access can be determinate by creating groups. [1]

B. Groups

- Admins are super users. They have full access and can manage lower tier users. Examples: system administrator, security administrator. [1]

- Managers maintain the content of the system, interact with user interface, upgrade and maintain content. Examples: content manages, web designer, webmaster. [1]

- Users are profiles without special privileges and their access level is the lowest. Users can access only highly specific content. Examples: registered user, intranet user, extranet user, unregistered user. [1]

C. Dynamic profiling

Standard user profiling can be extended by dividing users based on additional account criteria. This can be determined by implementing specific user case scenarios, monitoring user activity, data access, and redundancy of activities per each session. By taking all this data, profiles can be customized more individually, and user friendly. User interface can be customized for each profile's need and the same for the data access which results in higher interactivity and security of the system. [1]

PROFILE MANAGEMENT

A. Models

Over the years proper user profile management was a problem of many different segments of the market from websites, applications or large scale systems. The purpose was to create more comprehensive user experience. The problem of creating accurate profile and data mining was studied for years and in order to solve this dilemma there must be implemented a data model. A model that describes which information must be gathered in order to build profile fitting the business model of application. Next step is to create a profile model which is based on data model and describes behaviour and presents facts about user. Last thing is the construction of the profile by applying data mining algorithms in order to capture behaviors of the users. [2]

B. Example algorithms
- Apriori – discovers associations rules
- CART – classifications rules [2]

Although, algorithms and methods may vary from case to case, it greatly depends on what is the purpose of the applications or system. [2]

C. Implementation and validation

One of the last and the most important things is validation. From previously described models and algorithms, certain rules are being created and implemented into the system. In order to verify that algorithms are correct and profiles are accurate, a system has to be reinforced with validations rules that will manage information about profiles. [2]

A. Validation methods
- Template-based rule filtering – only rules that fit into the predefined template are validated
- Redundant rule elimination – operator which checks if rules are not redundant means that if a rule can satisfy some conditions there is no more rules that satisfy them as well
- Visualization operators – rejected rules are presented in different charts that administrator can manually accept rules that apply to the conditions
- Statistical analysis operator – presents many statistical vies about rules which gives administrator additional insight
- Browsing operator – gives administrator the opportunity to get inside the rule and inspect it manually [2]

PROFILES IN THE CLOUD

Recent years has shown that plenty of IT sector is migrating to the cloud environment including ERP systems. These changes have developed certain problems regarding moving data from stationary ERP systems into the cloud, namely maintaining proper security and data consistency. [3]

TABLE I. Migration [3]

Moving profiles to cloud		
Aspects	*Enterprise ERP*	*Cloud ERP*
Migration process	The amount of profiles (users) and how many servers are used to handle the traffic must be determined. Define the user differences and which servers they are using. Those steps are necessary to reduce downtime of the service and move only parts of the system.	Cloud service must be running along with enterprise while data is being moved. Therefore, before moving the data cloud service is taking care of the traffic and share information with enterprise system until the data is secured in cloud.
Security	All the traffic during the migration must be filtered with predefined rules which separate from unwanted traffic. Thanks to that, data is caught and redirected through firewalls to cloud.	In cloud there are additional rules that filter received data and redistribute to proper server.
Performace	Enterprise system must be measured and its performance must be determined in order to prepare cloud service of similar power. Special algorithms are applied here to create and test all the rules.	Cloud service must run in similar way that enterprise system in order to maintain all the operations without delays. Redistributed to sufficient amount of data centers.
Accesibility	Data should be accessible all the time for all profiles during the migration process because of its architecture, and backing up with the cloud service. While migrating server by server it should be considered that some of the servers are connected and then should be moved together to maintain consistency.	Data are shared with enterprise system. Users that are trying to access the service and their profile is already moved to cloud, then their session is operated already in the cloud without any difference in usage or performance.
Costs	Measure delays between parts of the enterprise systems and determine if it is reasonable to move part of the system, few components or the whole system.	Check the bandwidth usage and compare it with the enterprise system and determine if it is cheaper to use enterprise or move to cloud in terms of data usage.

SECURITY OR EASE OF USE

User profiling can be considered as a part of security of the systems because it locks the access to data and allows controlling the access. An individual user is an actor in the

ERP system and his ability of using it should be natural, easy and straightforward. Users should not feel that they are being restricted to only using certain resources, although in terms of secured systems they should not have a full access to resources excluded from their profile accessibility. [4]

A. Accessibility

Five roles of the accessing the system can be distinguished in depend upon the profile of the user. [4]

- Dismissed – user use the system as it is predefined and expected

- Manipulator – user needs to obeys rules and instructions given from the system

- Bureaucrat – user agrees with instructions given by the system, also they are not so strong as in the manipulator

- Consultant – user is able to choose different options of his action. User may suggest different solution than that proposed by the system

- Administrator – case where system has less influence on the user, gives some support but do not suggest solution

B. Design

Systems should be adapted to the situations they will be used and preferences of the users. Before the implementation, computer knowledge of the users should be measured and their expectations should be taken into account. Collecting such data will help with providing necessary assistance during the usage of such a system and provide information for creating even more detailed and accurate user profiles. [5]

- SUMMARY

User profiling is a powerful management tool for ERP systems. Gathering information and data about the users and capturing their behaviour is an excellent way to improve the system: create more adaptive user interfaces, and separate demanded from unneeded data. Programmers can create and secure systems as the users want them to be. Automated procedures and algorithms can constantly work on upgrading the system even after it has been deployed. There are numerous ways of distinguishing profiles. System and user interact with each other and they need to take a certain predefined role. Once role gives more power and flexibility to the user and in different role, system is taking more control and decides for the user. There are also more balanced profiles that are somewhere in between full user control and non-control. Summarizing, we provide a secure way of exchanging data between parties, users and data providers. Another important issue mentioned in the article is migration to the cloud; it is a highly complicated operation which needs a lot of preparations and tools, both before starting the process and afterwards. Though, it demands a lot on experience, tools, and predefined solutions, depends of the size of the system, scope, time and costs, different parts of the system must work while being moved to the cloud.

References

[1] Zykov, S. V., 2002. The Integrated Approach to ERP: Embracing the Web. *Proceedings of 4th International Workshop on Computer Science and Information Technologies,* pp. 4-5.

[2] Adomavicius, G. & Tuzhilin, A., 1999. User Profiling in Personalizat ion Applications through. *ACM,* pp. 377-380.

[3] Hajjat, M. et al., 2010. Cloudward Bound: Planning for Beneficial Migration of. *ACM,* pp. 243-53.

[4] Askenäs, L. & Westelius, A., 2000. FIVE ROLES OF AN INFORMATION SYSTEM :A SOCIAL CONSTRUCTIONIST APPROACH TO ANALYZING THE USE OF ERP SYSTEMS. *ACM,* pp. 431-433.

[5] Sia, S. K., Tang, M., Soh, C. & Boh, W. F., 2002. Enterprise Resource Planning (ERP) Systems as a Technology of Power: Empowerment or Panoptic Control?. *The DATA BASE for Advances in Information Systems,* pp. 26-28.

Key Challenges for Global Cloud ERP

Lew Kok Way

School of Computing and Mathematics
University of Derby
Derby, United Kingdom
k.lew1@unimail.derby.ac.uk

Abstract—**Presently many companies conduct business globally. These companies implement Enterprise Resource Planning (ERP) systems to support their operations. With the emergence of Cloud technology, this has further influenced the decision for worldwide deployment. Whilst Cloud based implementations may simplify the adoption of ERP, there are remaining a significant set of challenges to face which are mainly regional factors of legislation, culture and skill labour force. This article identifies the key challenges and the main contributory factors, suggesting a move towards best practice in the global implementation of Cloud based ERP.**

Keywords-ERP; Cloud; global implementation; challenges

INTRODUCTION

In recent years, ERP has gradually increased in popularity as a choice to facilitate corporations in managing information systems, which include accounting, manufacturing sales and customer relationship management (CRM). With the emerging delivery model of Cloud computing, ERP systems can now be integrated into the cloud platform for scalability and high availability. Such architectures can dramatically lower the start-up cost as well as ongoing IT costs. The nature of Cloud based ERP is high availability, that can be accessed from anywhere, making it a desirable choice for global implementation to leverage existing operations. It also eases a corporation in controlling worldwide operations by centrally coordinating the entire information system.

Nowadays, many companies are turning their businesses into global market by venturing into in other countries to expand their business. This can be done by having branches in different countries or having joint ventures with other multinational companies. With diversified businesses in many countries, a global ERP implementation is crucial to accommodate the daily operations to connect overseas branches, suppliers and customers. Customers' orders from around the world can be easily received by the system. Hence information can be gathered quickly and accurately to update the inventory system to replenish supply. This can avoid delays processes that would be costly to the business.

With the Cloud ERP system, it is easier for worldwide integration. Holland and Light (1999) mentioned that the increasing globalisation pressure has forced international organisations to improve the level of international economic co-ordination amongst national entities of the same firm. A standardised package of ERP solution is normally a choice of implementation in an environment of diversified offshore business units. However, business units often face certain difficulties during the implementation of ERP in foreign countries. This paper serves to identify the types of challenges faced by multinational companies in implementing ERP systems.

CLOUD ERP BACKGROUND

ERP systems have been used by many companies many years ago. The conventional ERP systems were normally implemented on the premise itself. The cost invested is not just on the ERP but also the hardware, software and network infrastructure that are needed to facilitate the ERP system. As a result, a company may require hiring a bigger IT team to support both the platform and system. In some cases, ERP vendors provide the whole package that includes managing the hardware platform on top of systems as it is harder to upgrade or change the platform.

With the ever increasing competitive market in providing ERP solutions, ERP systems providers are offering additional services that make their products more attractive than the others. One of the major improvements made is to integrate it with the latest emerging Cloud technology. Cloud providers offer three basic types of services which include Software as a Service (SaaS), Platform as a service (PaaS) and Infrastructure as a service (IaaS). Companies such as Saleforce.com are using SaaS in its delivery model. This allows ERP systems to be delivered to the users via the internet, thereby; eliminating the hardware platforms.

Table I shows the differences between conventional ERP systems and the Cloud based ERP systems.

TABLE V.

Differences	Conventional ERP vs Cloud based ERP	
	Conventional ERP	*Cloud based ERP*
Hardware platform	Systems are located on premise.	Systems are located on premise.
Cost	Very high upfront cost that require hardware, software, licenses and network infrastructure.	Much lower upfront cost without network infrastructure.
Skills	Only require skills on managing the ERP systems.	Maybe require skills on managing both ERP systems and Cloud platform, depending on vendor package.

Differences	Conventional ERP vs Cloud based ERP	
	Conventional ERP	*Cloud based ERP*
Availability	On premise ERP systems rely on the network infrastructure of the company. Poor network setup may cause downtime.	The cloud has a robust network and bandwidth that can be accessed anytime anywhere.
Scalability	Hardly scalable or may require very complicated process.	Cloud resources are highly scalable. Performance can be increased or decreased easily on demand.
Support	More manpower is required to support every part of the IT infrastructure.	The company does not require supporting the network, software and licenses.
Locality & Privacy	Data are stored on premise with lower network latency.	Data might be stored in different region with high network latency, depending on the provider. Data stored with provider might create privacy issue.
Time	The ERP systems installation is time consuming and require many phase of processes.	Cloud based ERP is ready to use anytime.

TYPES OF CHALLENGES

A. Cultural and language differences

According to the research by Sheu, Chae and Yang (2004), it was confusing for Chinese countries to key in names into the ERP system in the western format as they normally use surname as the first name while in western format, it would be reverse. As most of the ERP systems are developed to support only in the English language, this limitation has caused obstacles in data entry for most employees from the Asian counterparts. The different language between Asian and western countries has caused a big communication barrier. This forces employees to learn English which maybe relatively hard and time consuming for them. Thus, this leads to a resistance to change in adapting to the new ERP system.

Problems worsen when local employees are expected to maintain the system after being instigated by the headquarters. As the system is built on a different language, the IT department will have a hard time maintaining the system when errors occur. Consequently, they may start to install and maintain their own ERP system which suits better in the local environment. This may be beneficial in eradicating the current problem but this may backfire as decentralisation may cause inaccuracy in data.

The differences in the cultural behaviour between different continents or countries are also the cause of resistance. For example, the Chinese would normally practice taking orders via phone calls and without any proper contracts. This practise is considered unacceptable to the Westerners as formal documentation is always a basic and crucial requirement. Besides, English language is not the first language in most Asian companies; and hence they tend to ignore or delete any long emails or notice that they find hard to comprehend.

B. Format and Standardisation

In order to improve the overall information flow, multinational corporations tend to implement ERP system using global template in pursuing standardisation. With standardisation, these companies are able to maintain the structure and processes that will rule out complication during implementation. This can also avoid wasting time and effort in customizing the system for each branch in different countries. However, Hawking. P. (2007) argued that the extensive use of global templates cause lack of flexibility at the local level to take advantages of regional opportunities.

Every country has different type of reporting or accounting practice and standard. For example, SAP uses a standard where a decimal point is included in the currency unit. However, some Asian countries do not use any decimal format which has been rounded up or down to the nearest zero. Most of the time, the currency of these countries involve huge figure. A very good example is the Japanese Yen; the figure could go up to million or billion. The format differences for each country will cause ambiguities to ERP system users in the company.

The standardisation of ERP system configuration force employees to adopt a new way of operating processes. In most occasions, employees will refuse to change due to dissatisfaction claiming that this new way of process contradicts to the method they adopt in the country.

C. Governmental Diplomacy and Data Privacy

Every country has different policies or regulations such as tax requirement or document handling. Most of these regulations are formed to protect own country's sovereignty. Also, diplomatic relationships between countries do affect ERP system implementation. According to Sheu, Chae and Yang (2004), Taiwan and China have enforced some strict regulations on transporting goods, exchanging information or transferring money in between both countries. Other than these, every country has different set of custom forms and procedure or tariff rates.

A different tax rate on each country often causes complicated implementation. Normally, the companies will try to develop a way to reduce or avoid whatever taxes involved. As a result, there is a need to come up with complex ERP system to adapt to the operating procedure requirement. Other than that, different formats in legal documentations such as invoices would also affect ERP implementation. Such disparity and restriction would force a company to make drastic customization in order to satisfy individual standard and requirement.

Data privacy is a big concern since ERP system uses the Cloud as a platform. Different legislations in each country offer different level of data privacy. In certain countries such as the United States, data stored in servers that reside in the country and its territories are subject to the PATRIOT Act that allows the authorities to intercept communication. This issue has raised doubt among companies on whether to adopt ERP system because they have no idea where the data is stored by their ERP provider. Many are sceptical and refuse to use the system, worrying that the system itself might leak data to their rivals.

D. Labour Skills

In some less developed countries, many local companies are still practise paper filing and documentation. Foreign investors that expand their investment into these countries are finding it hard to implement ERP system since most employees in these countries are computer illiterate. These employees will need basic training to operate a computer, not to mention handling the more sophisticated ERP system.

With Cloud as a platform in ERP implementation, it means taking care of the system becomes more complicated. Since the ERP system heavily depends on the network infrastructure, constant monitoring is crucial to achieve high availability. However, this will require highly skilled worker to look after the company's network infrastructure. Employees in developing countries may not come aware of the existence of Cloud technology, and without proper training, it is almost impossible to look after the system.

E. Geographical and Infrastructure

Cloud based ERP system heavily relies on internet connection. The Cloud provides services the entire day and night to all different regions and countries via internet. Therefore, the companies' network infrastructures are very important to ensure the reliability and availability of data communication. Usually, these companies are reluctant to pay more in upgrading their network infrastructure after investing a large sum of money implementing the ERP system. Poor network setup or inferior network devices will cause intermittent disruptions that will cause data corruption. For companies that are located in remote locations or suburban area, network backbone infrastructure for the area may be underdeveloped or undeveloped. This means lower bandwidth and therefore, this creates network bottlenecks.

Meanwhile, different regions have significantly different regional time that could affect the international operation. For instance, 12 noon in Kuala Lumpur, Malaysia means 12 midnight in New York, United States. It is very difficult for both sides to conduct video conferences when something important arises. Other than that, differences in currency and the frequent changes in foreign exchange could also affect the trading operation.

CONCLUSION AND BEST PRACTICE

Global implementation of ERP systems is essential for many companies in order to ensure smooth information flow, especially companies that are expanding their business overseas. It provides a structured support for global operation and integration to the organisation. By using Cloud based ERP systems, centralization of data and information are made easier and efficient. However, implementation faces numerous challenges such as geographical and cultural differences that complicate the implementation process. Often people are afraid to change or to use ERP systems because they are not willing to learn new things.

However all this can be changed if the system is made simple or is user friendly. The flexibility of the ERP systems should allow easy integration or customization. The ERP vendors should increase the functionality with more option choices that cover different countries and come up with new version release of template to adopt different formats. They can establish a global websites to receive feedbacks from users on areas to improve.

Studying the background of each country before implementing the ERP systems can provide more accurate results for easier adaptation and adoption. Spending more effort on customising the ERP systems will make the systems suitable for global implementation. This also means it is much better than a complete disaster in the end which may cost even more. Selecting the right employee and hiring multilingual local team leaders will encourage better communication flow that will help avoid communication confusion and breakdown.

REFERENCES

[1] C. Sheu, B. Chae, C. Yang, "National differences and ERP Implementation: issues and challenges," Department of Management, College of Business Administration, Kansas State University, Manhattan, 2004. (references)

[2] P. Hawking, "Implementing ERP System Globally: Challenges and Lessons Learned for Asian Countries," Journal of Business Systems, Vol 2, No. 1, 2007.

[3] S. Ghosh, "Challenges on a global implementation of ERP software," Engineering Management Conference, Vol 2, 2002.

[4] S. Ghosh, "Global implementation of ERP software – critical success factors on upgrading technical infrastructure," Engineering Management Conference, 2003.

Cloud-based ERP: the risk of vendor lock-in

Matthew Burns
School of Computing and Mathematics
University of Derby
Derby, United Kingdom
m.burns2@unimail.derby.ac.uk

Abstract— Generally, organisations seeking to outsource cloud-based ERP are inadvertently prone to focus on the business and operational advantages this solution offers. However, with the cloud becoming an increasingly complex environment for organisations to manage their operations and processes within, it is important that the risks involved in cloud-based solutions are regarded as a significant concern by organisations. This paper discusses an emerging issue within the cloud environment - vendor lock-in – with deliberation on the types of lock-in situations organisations may inadvertently be faced with and reasons as to why these circumstances arise. Also included is discussion on the effects of this issue within the cloud and the problems that lack of cloud computing standardisation creates for organisations seeking cloud service solutions.

Keywords- cloud-computing; lock-in; ERP; vendor; customer

INTRODUCTION

It is now clearly evident that cloud-based Enterprise Resource Planning (ERP) systems provide organisations with an operationally and cost effective solution to managing particular processes within their business. Once moved into the cloud, organisations become empowered to increase their capabilities and business competitiveness through the use of the core models of cloud-based services without the need to invest in new or further Information Systems/Information Technology (IS/IT) infrastructure; including servers, hardware, software, and security measures. Additionally, in concurrence with the expansion of the infrastructure, investment in human resource and training is not always required. This is greatly beneficial for those organisations with limited capabilities in particular; perhaps lacking IT budget, infrastructure and expertise to justify in-house systems. However, for businesses planning to move their ERP systems into the cloud, or even those seeking development of their existing cloud-based systems, through outsourcing, challenges and issues arise due to the intricate nature of the service provider-client relationship. One major consequence of these intricacies can occur; unforeseen lock-in situations where customers become inadvertently dependent on their vendors, with little room for flexibility with their new, or developed, cloud environment. The convenience of cloud computing has and continues to power its increasing popularity, but with that there comes an increasing concern of vendor control among customers [1]. As cloud services have been adopted during the technology's development, it has become clear there is a genuine problem as far as customers of cloud services are concerned, because of incompatible proprietorial solutions.

CLOUD ENVIRONMENT

Significantly, there is an apparent lack of overall governance and standardisation of service interoperability and the formal procedures to follow during the process of revising vendor-customer agreements or situations where customers require alteration to their cloud-based solutions. This absence of dominion over the cloud-computing environment, in most cases, creates opportunity for vendors to ultimately dictate their client's post-contract operation and activity within the cloud. This problem is a consequence of the fact that cloud computing still remains an emerging technology; with rapid growth of development and adoption it has not been feasible for standards to be devised to govern vendor-customer discrepancies. As a result, organisations are vulnerable of becoming overly dependent on their vendor. Ultimately, organisations require a constant and suitable service, and depend on their vendors to provide it. But a substantial degree of customer independence helps in mitigating the risk of becoming locked-in with service providers. In some cases, organisations may not necessarily see this reliance as an immediate cause for concern, as they may have assessed their vendors as suitable service providers to support their business interests and operations from a long-term perspective. Even then, their contentment to remain with their providers may eventually fade out; perhaps when unforeseen business and IS/IT environments and requirements change.

RISK ASSESSMENT

Cloud-based ERP systems pose numerous risks for organisations, primarily concerning issues involving information security; but at a business continuity level, vendor lock-ins should be considered within the overall risk assessment of cloud-based ERP systems. The European Network and Information Security Agency (ENISA) identify vendor lock-in as a significant risk to organisations [2]. ENISA evaluates the risk of vendor lock-in as one of high probability with medium impact levels. Of course, circumstance plays a part in the level of lock-in impact on organisations. In the very worst-case scenarios, cloud-computing vendors may cease to exist, or become administered as a result of filing for bankruptcy, leaving organisations that rely on their services with major business continuity issues. Within the report, ENISA identifies the vulnerabilities within the vendor-customer relationship and their functionality between each other that can result in lock-in situations. Indeed a lack of standard technologies and unification of interfaces within the cloud stack creates barriers for migration. Organisational data is the primary asset at risk from lock-in situations. If data cannot be migrated, accessed or retrieved by the organisation because of the lack of interoperability at the individual levels of the cloud stack, business continuity is at risk. In conjunction with risks to organisational data, vendor lock-in creates an issue of dependency. If migration is not immediately feasible, poor provider selection may lead to loss of data due to insufficient security measures at the service provider's end, or even downtime. This, of course, can be regulated through means of Service-Level Agreements (SLAs), but contractual obligations do not necessarily guarantee an impervious and stable service. If an organisation becomes dissatisfied with their vendor's services, or the vendor goes out of business, it is not always feasible to transfer services or migrate back to in-house. The organisation would need to reformat the schema to transfer them to a new provider who can support the new coding if they choose a new vendor, or even bringing the solution back to in-house would require investment in personnel capable of managing the new system [3].Furthermore to the ENISA findings; Papazoglou and van den Heuvel [4] indicate that analysts conducted studies that revealed vendor lock-in and undeveloped interoperability standards is deemed a bigger objection for cloud migration than even security concerns.

CIRCUMSTANCE

Lock-in situations are ultimately when a customer is tied in with a vendor contract and their services. Organisations purchase cloud-based services as a product from a supplier, only to then eventually be faced with an over dependency on that product and their vendor, with substantial migration costs that would break them free from the lock-in.In the current cloud climate, data, applications and services are primarily vulnerable to the risk of lock-in. Database schemas, data formats andapplication programming interfaces (APIs) are valuable in providing the function of interoperability of communication and processing within the cloud. However, the 'closed' proprietorial coding of these key components results in the need for resource (human, time and cost) to be focused into developing a solution to break free from being locked into solutions with particular platforms and languages.There is a range of circumstance that can result in vendor lock-in situations, most often broken down into situations regarding interoperability, or lack of. These circumstances translate into particular types of vendor lock-in, which affect the core services within the cloud environment (or 'stack'); Infrastructure-as-a-Service (IaaS), Platform-as-a-Service (Paas) and Software-as-a-Service (SaaS).

A. Horizontal Lock-In

Horizontal lock-in occurs when vendors restrict their customers to freely replace a service with a similar or competitive product. This situation can arise when a customer wishes to move to another solution but there are migration limitations put in place upon them by their vendor; affecting the ease of data portability, training end users and re-creation of cloud-based to on-premises integration.

Provided there is a clear plan for the migration process, SaaS solution change is generally implementable. Change in PaaS is more difficult to achieve due to the lack of interoperability between language platforms as an underlying infrastructure of the proprietor architecture. IaaS horizontal lock-in situations are more manageable; in that they are mitigated through use of hypervisor based virtual machines isolating hardware differences, allowing relative ease of workload distribution.

B. Vertical Lock-In

A vertical lock-in situation can be seen as when customers are restricted to the use of specific software and hardware within the overall cloud service stack as a result of a chosen solution. Use of operating system, database, hardware supplier and even any required implementation partner during migration may be dictated by the vendor. At a SaaS and PaaS level, vertical lock-in situations can be somewhat difficult to avoid, since the choice and location of hardware at the data centre is out of their control. Consistent calibration of wide scale systems is key to the business model of cloud-based service providers; resulting in customers having to unfortunately justify extra costs that will arise to develop solutions for new operability between the components of the stack architecture.

C. Inclined Lock-In

Sometimes referred to as 'diagonal' vendor lock-in, inclined lock-in arises when organisations freely choose the provision of numerous services within the stack from a single provider, even if there are better alternatives out there on the market for each particular service. Demand of discount due to this 'one-stop shop' approach drives down provision costs, but further increases vendor control over the customer's future operability within the cloud.

D. Generational Lock-In

This type of lock-in arises when inevitably solutions and platforms die out due to their lack of interoperability with the more up-to-date cloud technologies. A generational lock-in situation is likely to arise if an organisation adopts solutions provided by those vendors who are not necessarily capable of becoming the leaders, perhaps even dictators, of the development of the cloud environment and the services incorporated within it. This circumstance is eventually unavoidable at all levels of the cloud stack; the problem organisations face is that the use of vendor's cloud-based services may support their short term interests, however at some point older solutions will prove incompatible with further developed or perhaps completely new cloud paradigms.

CAUSES

These types of vendor lock-in can affect the levels of the cloud stack due to specific circumstances; it is because of proprietorial coding, it is ultimately the deficiency in API and data schema interoperability that results in the locking-in of specific services. Incompatible code results in the inability to achieve portability of data, application and services; with time and money required to justify the development of a separate API to rectify the problem. Even then this newly developed APIs functionality is limited as it is locked into specific interfaces. Rudimentary examples of why the aforementioned types of lock-in may occur within the three core levels of the cloud stack are indicated in Table I.

TABLE VI.   EXAMPLES OF VENDOR LOCK-IN

Lock-in type	Service level		
	IaaS	*PaaS*	*SaaS*
Horizontal	Provision of a specific infrastructure services can only support a particular operating system.	An underlying virtualisation platform cannot function with newer APIs.	Data or an application cannot be migrated to another provider due to incompatibility.
Vertical	The underlying infrastructure of a cumulated solution through the stack limits future interoperability.	Database services cannot be migrated to a different virtualisation platform.	Migration of an application is dependent on the use of an undesired operating system.
Inclined	Application and software development becomes dependent on the flexibility of the infrastructure being provided by the vendor.	A better runtime environment solution cannot be implemented due to the homogeneous operability of the sole vendor's service.	An organisation that relies on a sole provider cannot change an application service due to the incompatibility of the wanted service.
Generational	An organisation's new data schema is not interoperable with an older storage service.	An older API cannot function within a newer platform it is needs to function upon.	Data on an older schema cannot be processed through new API technologies, as it has been rendered obsolete.

THE VENDOR PERSPECTIVE

There is an increasing concern within organisations considering migration to the cloud that they will become too dependent on the wrong solution [5], resulting in lock-in; but from the point of view of the vendors offering cloud services, they are dependent on the exploitation of a closed cloud environment. As of now, standardisation of cloud APIs

has not been put in place meaning they are still proprietary to those who provide them. From a vendor point of view, standardisation of APIs would inadvertently result in cloud service providers seeking to find means of driving down their service costs, ergo operating costs, in order to obtain a substantial market share. This would arise due to the unification of APIs creating absolute interoperability within the cloud stack, leaving customers freedom to effectively 'roam' within the cloud as they please. Simply put, this lack of lock-in would not enable providers to maintain a customer base and compete within the industry; quite possibly resulting in complete monopolisation of the cloud environment by the market leaders.

There are numerous initiatives being carried out (including 'OpenCloud', 'Open Cloud Initiative' and 'OpenStack') that focus on the delivery of open service layer solutions, creating a scalable and elastic cloud service. These initiatives are an effort from both major and minor cloud computing organisations to push for standards and cloud interoperability, motivated by the will to stabilise and protect the future of the cloud computing paradigm.

CONCLUSIONS

As discussed within this article, vendor lock-in is a key concern for organisations seeking to migrate to the cloud for their ERP solutions, because of the proprietorial cloud-based data schemas and APIs. With immature standardisation of the cloud environment and the interoperability within the cloud stack, there lies an obvious problem that will take time to rectify to the point in which customers and vendors coexist efficiently within the cloud environment; whilst ensuring the cloud is maintained as a platform for operations, a technological paradigm, a market, an industry and a business environment.

Market leader's support of the existing initiatives seeking to open up the cloud will prove significant in maintaining it, as on a greater scale, there is potential that a lingering lack of standardisation running in parallel with the further development of new cloud technologies will see increasing levels of interoperability; resulting in organisations reverting to in-house solutions. This could eventually break down the cloud as even a loosely unified platform in which businesses can operate within, as organisations become demotivated to use the cloud to support their business operations.

Through loss of custom fears and flexibility of service appealing to customers, cloud service providers should be motivated to proactively seek means to interoperate with each other maintaining an open cloud through sufficient data and application portability. In the meantime organisations would be wise to assess their service providers carefully, with significant consideration for the long term future and factoring in costs involved in migration or reverting back to their in-house solution.

ACKNOWLEDGMENT

Thank you to Dr. Richard Hill, (University of Derby, Derby, United Kingdom) for his guidance and my academic peers for their supporting research.

REFERENCES

[1] Briscoe, G. and Marinos, A., "Digital Ecosystems in the Clouds: Towards Community Cloud Computing", in 3rd IEEE International Conference on Digital Ecosystems and Technologies, 2009, p. 104.

[2] European Network and Information Security Agency, "Cloud Computing: Benefits, Risks and Recommendations for Information Security", 2009, pp.25-28.

[3] Leavitt, N., "Is Cloud Computing Really Ready for Prime Time?", in IEEE Computer Society: Technology News 2009, pp.18-19.

[4] Papazoglou, P.M., and van den Heuvel, W-J., "Blueprinting the Cloud", in IEEE Internet Computing: View from the Cloud, 2011, p. 75.

[5] Blake, J. and Borenstein, N., "Cloud Computing Standards: Where's the Beef?", in IEEE Internet Computing: Standards, 2011, p. 75

Analysis of cloud security in relation to ERP

Michael Heaton
School of Business computing and Law
University of Derby
Derby, Derbyshire

Abstract— **Moving to a cloud based ERP system can offer many benefits such as, reduced costs and improved efficiency. However with any new technology there are always security issues that need to be analyzed and weighed up before committing to the change. If these issues are overlooked it could lead to loss of sensitive information.**

This paper will look at what security concerns potentiality exists within the cloud and how these concerns will affect any cloud ERP system. Finally this paper will discuss prospective countermeasures that can be enforced to reduce any risk of a security breach.

Keywords-component; Cloud Computing; ERP; Security;

INTRODUCTION

Cloud computing is a new up and coming technology that offers many advantages for all kinds of situations. ERP systems have started to shift towards the cloud as it offers many benefits for any business that utilizes them. However with all the benefits that cloud computing offers there are security issues that need to be addressed.

A large part of security is the trust between the client and the provider. The service level agreement, (SLA) is the legal agreement between the two parties. The SLA is the only way that the provider can gain the trust of the client so therefore it has to be standardized.

This paper will look at cloud computing security in relation to ERP, and discuss how they could affect any cloud ERP system. Secondly since the SLA is important in building trust and setting security guidelines between the two parties this paper will discuss SLA's and ways they can be improved. Finally this paper will look at some security measures that can be used to counter these security threats.

CLOUD COMPUTING

Cloud computing is a means which allows scalable services to be used over the Internet on demand. [1]. It is also a means for anyone to access resources from any location at any time without having to worry about having to manage any hardware and maintenance issues. [2]

As stated by [3] cloud computing can be implemented in three main styles which are software as service (SaaS), platform as a service (PasS) and infrastructure as a service (IaaS). SaaS and IaaS are mainly for development purposes and are not that relevant to this paper. SaaS on the other hand is very relevant for ERP systems as it allows users to access many forms of software on their local machine a key example of this is Google docs.

Cloud computing also has a massive effect on the implementation on ERP systems as it gives a new platform for which it can be used. Cloud computing ERP also allows small to medium businesses to utilize an ERP system as traditional ERP implementations cost more than most businesses can afford.

Vendors are starting to adapt to the need for cloud ERP systems. For example Lawson and Compier have both released a ERP systems based on Amazon EC2. However most noticeably in 2010 Japan's Nec went into partnership with SAP to create a powerful cloud based ERP system [4].

However even though there are many cloud ERP vendors and taking into account all the benefits there are still security issues with cloud ERP systems that this paper will address.

SERVIVE LEVEL AGREEMENT

The SLA is a contract which defines the primary relationship between the cloud computing provider and the customer. If the contract is used correctly it should identify a wide range of things from what the customer's needs are, to reducing complex areas.

The SLA does not affect any ERP systems directly; it does however affect any cloud service it is hosted on, as a poorly written SLA can lead to the ERP system being vulnerable to a variety of attacks.

One of the most important areas of the SLA as stated by [] is security, in this section the customer must state what physical and logical security they are putting in place to help strengthen security. Also this section should state that the provider should respect the security polices the customer has in place.

The majority of cloud providers use waivers as a way to avoid the customer taking legal action against them if they fail to live up to expectations. So therefore this current system does not help the customer in anyway.

This paper will discuss some ways that SLA's can be improved to increase the level of trust that the customers have that there data will be secure. If the following sections are written into the SLA the customer will feel protected against any event.

The cloud provider should provide a section within the SLA on recovery, this section should describe what would happen to the customers data and service in case of a disaster. If this question is not clarified the customer is risking total failure.

Cloud services are very difficult to investigate since customer data may be spread over many locations and therefore many illegal actives may go unnoticed, the provider needs to state that they will support these forms of investigation.

A very important topic that needs to be covered in the SLA is what happens if the cloud provider goes into administration or gets acquired by larger company. The SLA needs to state that the information must available after such an event, if that is not possible there must be a contingency plan in place to ensure that the customer has access to all their data.

CLOUD SECURITY ISSUES

This paper will now look at the top cloud computing security threats.

TABLE I

1. Server setup.	A test completed by [1] which analyzed the firewalls in cloud computing setups indicated that 50% of cases they were setup incorrectly. An incorrectly set up firewall could allow a potential hacker access to the ERP system and potential critical business information.
2.Insecure API's	Many cloud computing providers give their customers access to a set of interfaces []. These APIs handle all forms of security from authentication to encryption, if these APIs happen to be weak it opens up the cloud system to all forms of attack. Therefore comprising any information stored within an ERP system.
3.Malicious Insiders	Every computing system is vulnerable to malicious insiders and cloud computing is no exception. The damage that a malicious insider can do is substantial as they will have access to every piece of sensitive information on the ERP system and henceforth be able to inflict all kinds of damage. [7]
4.Account Hacking	This was recognized by [7] as being a top threat, as stolen user credentials allow an attacker into the most critical areas of the cloud computing system as well as the ERP system.
5. Jurisdiction where data is held.	The majority of users of cloud services do not know where their information is being held [6] even though the EU have very strict privacy laws, other countries such as America with the patriot act allow the government almost limitless power to access even the most sensitive information. Therefore if a server is within a non EU country with a cloud ERP system and is raided, all that information is potentially no longer secure.
6. Privacy/ Data Protection	Since a business's sensitive information is not stored on their computers, data protection is a main concern. Furthermore there is another concern that the provider may unlawfully use the data stored on the server for unlawful gains. A survey done by [8] indicated that 90% cloud users are very concerned that their data might be sold on by the provider. This is ever more prominent with ERP systems, as said systems contain all sorts of sensitive of information that businesses can't afford to lose.

a. Cloud security issues

There are measures that can be put in place to counteract the security threats mentioned. Such when it comes to the server setup, the only solution is that before the server goes live, the provider should simulate a variety of attacks, and therefore make sure that all the security software is setup correctly.

Another measure that can be put in place to help prevent the issue of insecure API's, is to analyze the security model that the cloud provider uses for its interfaces. As by analyzing the security models this would ensure, that before any ERP system is implemented that the API's have been checked for any vulnerabilities and therefore potentially avoid any major security breaches.

Furthermore a measure that be used to help prevent the problem of malicious insiders is to use a technology called trusted cloud computing platform (TTCP). [7] TTCP provides a closed environment which means each customer will have access to virtual machines (VM's) to store their data and applications. This does not allow the provider's administrator's access to any specific VM which could potentially reduce the threat of a malicious insider dramatically.

To prevent the issue of account hijacking the cloud provider has to enforce strict regulations to minimize the risk. One of the best solutions as identified by [6] is for the cloud provider to use two factor authentication, which means that every user needs to enter something they own with their password such as fingerprints or a ID cards. Therefore if a hacker gets hold of a user password it will be much harder to break into the cloud service as well as ERP system.

Finally the only way at the moment to handle jurisdiction laws is to know where the information is held. The customer ideally needs some form of written confirmation of where the data is held, the SLA is the perfect place to do this. All providers in Europe have guidelines set out by the council of Europe. The document that sets out these guidelines is called the 'convention of cybercrime'. The purpose of the article is to establish a level of extraterritorial jurisdiction. This makes it easier to determine who is legally responsible for any information technology offences. The document can give the customer some piece of mind as there are laws that can protect them. If the provider is in a non EU country they are not protected by these guidelines and therefore the customer are assuming an unnecessary risk with their data.

CONCLSUION

Cloud based ERP systems offer many benefits to any business that implements one; however this paper has shown cloud computing needs much more work before it achieves a promising level of security. This paper has focused on cloud security threats, it has explained some possible solutions that if implemented can reduce risk, however this does not guarantee complete data security.

This paper has also shown that selection of the cloud provider is fundamental, as a trusted provider can ensure a higher level of security as they will have extensive experience in dealing with a wide range of issues. Secondly they will also have a well written SLA as well as being based within a trusted jurisdiction.

To conclude, this paper has shown that even though ERP systems are trusted and reasonably secure, cloud ERP systems at the moment are not completely. However with all the advancement being made in the field of IT security there is promise that in the future that cloud based ERP could be better/equal to non-cloud ERP systems.

REFERENCES

[1]M.Jensen and J.Schwenk On Technical Security Issues in Cloud Computing" 2009
[2] F.B Shaikh and S.Haider "Security Threats in Cloud Computing" 2011
[3] Rajan.S, and Jairath.A Cloud computing the fifth generation of computing" 2011
[4] C.McKenna "Cloud and open source ERP". 2010
[5]Cloud security alliance "Top Threats to cloud computing" 2010
[6] D.Catteddu and G.Hogben "Cloud Computing security and risk assessment" 2009
[7] Rocha.F and M.Correia Lucy in the Sky without Diamonds. Stealing confidential data in the cloud, 2008
[8]Martin.C Jutstridictal aspects of cloud computing, 2009

Managing Dirty Data during ERP Systems Integration

Martin Smith

School of Computing and Mathematics

University of Derby

Derby, UK

martin.smith1982@hotmail.co.uk

Abstract---This article will investigate ways to find and clean up dirty data when merging old data into a new system. It will explore the problems of converting data that is stored as a JSON encoded string into XML when the JSON data has large amounts of dirty data.

Keywords; dirty data, data management, data problems, converting data types, testing.

BACKGROUND

A. Dirty Data

Dirty data is inaccurate, incomplete or inconsistent data that is stored in a system as part of a database or file [1]. As much as 25 percent of critical data in large organizations is dirty [2]. In the past dirty data only affected the system it was stored in due to most Information Technology (IT) systems being isolated and used to address specific problems [1]. However IT systems now operate 24 hours a day and are interconnected with many other systems sharing their data both clean and dirty [1]. Organizations have started to recognize the value of their data as an important asset and started to consolidate it into data warehouse and federated systems, however dirty data is hampering some efforts to this [3].

Dirty data is often data that is misspelled, missing information or just invalid, if the database holding the data is part of a multiple data source such as a data warehouse or federated system then it will affect much more than just the system it was entered in [4].

Single-source dirty data generally occurs when users enter data incorrectly such as spelling mistakes or inputting incorrect data whilst multi-source problems occur when data from different systems is represented differently, contradicts or is replicated when the data is merged [4].

Historically the quality control of data has been a desirable but low priority during development and maintenance of a system, once time or budget becomes tight it is one of the first activities to be neglected [1].

Dirty data can cause many problems for customer focused systems as incorrect or missing data could hinder sales attempts or make it harder to find potential business [2].

One of the largest reasons for dirty data continuing to exist in a system is that is not known about, identifying dirty data is difficult if undocumented changes have been made to a system or the original developer has left the organization [1], its only when a problem occurs because of dirty data that any action is taken and by then it could be too late. Even if dirty data is detected it's not always easy to correct it, software tools would have to be custom made to deal with the specific problem which could be costly and only work on that problem [1].

B. Problems of Dirty Data

Dirty data can have a negative impact on systems by having an effect on stock levels, orders and customer details all of which can impact the businesses reputation and profitability [1]. Data is used to make decisions, the dirty it is the less reliable any decisions will be that are made from it [5].

The Gartner Group [1] has identified several problem areas caused by dirty data, they claim that a significant amount of data integration and IT projects run over their budgets or fail completely due to data quality. They also mention large overheads due to poorly targeted mailings due to incorrect data in stored customer detail data. Another area where dirty data is causing problems is in Business Intelligence (BI) projects where it is essential to have clean data to produce accurate BI based decisions [1].

Dirty data can be defined as the following [3];

- Corrupted Data
- Duplicate Data
- Incorrect Data
- Incorrect Type
- Missing Data

If a dataset contains a high proportion of dirty data it will become unusable, with less a system will still be usable but might sometimes show incorrect data, if the system knows the exactly how the data should be formed then in some cases it can ignore bad data that does not match what's expected otherwise the only way to protect against it is to find and remove it [3].

Data is a valuable asset to an organization and should be treated as such, if the data is not consistent and accurate it de-values it worth to the organization and can lead to bad decision making and loss of confidence in the system [1]. Also once data loses its integrity it might be impossible to recover forcing data stewards to delete it [5].

A symptom of dirty data is a demoralized development team, if their work is hampered by poor data quality they will be slowed down and unable to perform as expected [1].

INVESTIGATION

A. Methods to Manage Dirty Data

Methods to manage dirty data should make sure that the data is accurate, consistent, complete and if possible to validate it [1].

The first step in managing dirty data is to audit the data, this involves searching through the data looking for discrepancies such as missing data or unexpected results [1]. Once dirty data has been found the next step is to clean the data, strip out anything that should not be there and attempt to make sense of it and format it as required, any discrepancies that can't be resolved should be flagged for human intervention [1]. The third step is prevention, there is no point correcting dirty data if it is still able to enter the system, this would involve auditing user input and validating data before storing it [1]. The fourth stage is to make sure that the format used to store the data is future proof and compatible with other systems [1], storing as XML would be one way to meet this step.

Other methods to manage dirty data could be to employ data stewards, they would make sure all data is accurate before it's entered into any systems [2] and technical solutions that could detect if data was formatted correctly.

There are various tools available to help with managing dirty data. Data analysis and reengineering tools are used for profiling and mining data, profiling tools check attributes and values whilst mining tools search for relationships amongst attributes. They are used to audit data to make sure it is correct [4].

Specialized cleaning tools are used to try and correct dirty data, they use rules provided in advance from a library or interactively from a user [4]. They try to automate the correction process but sometimes the data is unrecoverable.

Extract, Transform, Load (ETL) tools are used to validate data being entered into multiple-source systems, they make sure that incoming data does not conflict with any already stored, some of these tools also analyze and cleanup data before storing it [4].

B. Testing of data management methods

For testing we will use a dataset of 100 customer detail records, 33 of which will be dirty data. We will try and recover as much as possible using the audit, clean and compatibility steps. The data will stored in JSON strings using a separate table to define what each value in the string represents. This will mimic an old solo based system, we will then need to convert from JSON to XML so the data is compatible with new systems with zero dirty data.

Table 2 Current data format

Value 1	Value 2	Value 3	Value 4	Value 5	Value 6
First name	Last name	Phone	Post code	Street	Contacted

Table 1 shows the format of the current version of the systems JSON encoded strings, and extra value was added after the system went live to accommodate the customer's street name.

Table 3 Original data format

Value 1	Value 2	Value 3	Value 4	Value 5
First name	Last name	Phone	Post code	Contacted

Table 2 holds the original format for the JSON strings, luckily for us this was documented as part of the development notes so we are able to compare dirty data against it and make a safe conversion to XML. There have also been a few undocumented changes made to the format during the years that we will not be able to compensate for.

["Teagan","Rodriquez","1 91 788 7297-9920","MA5 6YT","3078 Faucibus Rd.","1"],

Figure 1 The JSON string of a customer.

Figure 1 shows a customer's record formatted in a JSON string, all data is held in the legacy system like this, to identify what a value is it must be compared with a heading table, shown here in table 1. This method can cause problems when sharing data with other systems as it would need to share the header as well, also if the header change and historic data will become dirty.

```
<customer>
<firstname>Teagan</firstname>
<secondname>Rodriquez</secondname>
<phone>1 91 788 7297-9920</phone>
<postcode>MA5 6YT</postcode>
<street>3078 Faucibus Rd.</street>
<contacted>1</contacted>
</customer>
```

Figure 2 Data formatted as XML

Figure 2 shows what the data will look like once it's converted to XML, in this format it's much easier to share with other systems as a description for what each value is built into it meaning there is no confusing about what a value represents. The only way for XML to become dirty is if the wrong values are placed in an attribute.

To test the auditing, cleaning and conversion steps we have built test using PHP and customer data in a JSON string. Figure 3 shows how the testing will be carried out, first we audit the data to see if it matches the current systems formatting, if it does it will be converted to XML, if not it will be cleaned by comparing it against historic data formats that we are aware have been used in the system in the past. If we can find a match the data is converted into XML else it's flagged for human intervention.

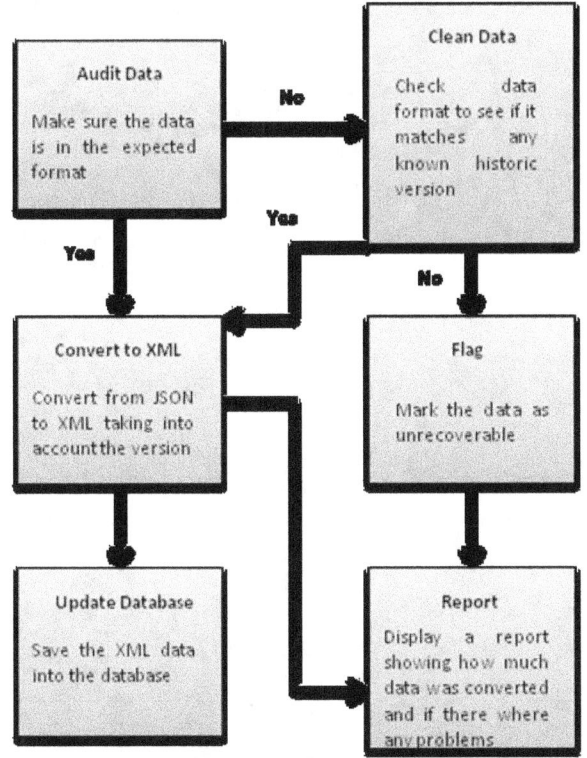

Figure 3 Data management method being used

The test was completed successfully by using the method described in Figure 3. We looped through all the data sets and managed to convert most of them to XML.

```
100 records Audited
Converted: 94 (Dirty: 27)
Failed: 6
```

Figure 4 Test results

Figure 4 shows that only 6 records out of the 100 failed to be converted, this was due to not having enough information available about what its values represented, these were also the records that used a data format that was never placed in the development notes.

By following the data management methods described earlier we were successful at saving as much data as possible, even wit human intervention it would be very difficult to decipher what the values actually mean for the 6 failed record sets as their format does not match anything known.

CONCLUSION

Dirty data is a major problem in systems integration that does not seem to be treated with the seriousness it deserves, data is valuable to organizations yet it's only recently that they are making an effort to protect their systems from dirty data. The more dirty data in a system the harder it will be to recover it and the less useful the entire data store will be due to its unreliability.

The methods for managing dirty data are efficient and can prevent most of it ever entering a system, however before fixing data the source of the problem needs to be found and fixed otherwise for every data record cleaned several more might get into the system.

With awareness slowly rising about dirty data we should start to see more measures in place to prevent and correct it which will hopefully not be abandoned once a projects budget starts running low or time starts to become short.

The testing that we carried out shows that dirty data can be saved if past system changes or documented, the more information we have the easier it is to reconstruct data into a usable format. We also showed that XML is a good format for data as it describes what its value is making it easy to understand what it's for and share with other systems.

By following good data management methods a systems data store should remain clean and efficient meaning employees and customers will have more trust in it and any decision the system has to make will be more accurate, it will also make integrating with new systems hassle free as the data would be stored in a share friendly format with no errors.

Good data management means an organization can keep its good reputation, show correct stock levels in their inventors and stores and to be able to successfully target new revenue opportunities.

REFERENCES

[1] R. Marsh, "Drowning in dirty data? It's time to sink or swim: A four-stage methodology for total data quality management," *Database Marketing & Customer Strategy Management vol 12,* pp. 105-112, 2005.

[2] A. Bitterer, "Gartner Warns Firms of 'Dirty Data'," *The Information Management Journal, May/June,* p. 6, 2007.

[3] W. Kim, C. Byoung, H. Eui-kyeong, K. Soo-kyung and L. Doheon, "A Taxonomy of Dirty Data," *Data Mining and Knowledge Discovery,* vol. 7, pp. 81-99, 2003.

[4] E. Rahm, "Data Cleaning: Problems and Current Approaches," *IEEE Data Engineering Bulletin 23,* pp. 3-13, 2000.

[5] J. Vosburg and A. Kumar, " Managing dirty data in organizations using ERP: lessons from a case study," *Industrial Management & Data Systems,* vol. 101, no. 1, p. 21, 2001.

Considerations for the use of Linked Server Databases for Cloud ERP

Nicholas Bosworth

School of Computing and Mathematics

University of Derby, UK

n.bosworth1@unimail.derby.ac.uk

Abstract—**SQL based database applications benefit from the ability to consume or provide resources to other compatible databases via Linked Server. When looking to migrating an ERP system to a cloud based solution the advantages and disadvantages of the Linked Server method should be considered in relation to the requirements of the enterprise. This paper examines whether the simple, performant and reactive configuration approach of Linked Servers for database to database communication should be preferred to the more future proof, secure and fail safe methods offered by alternative solutions. This is concluded with scenario aware recommendations as to which option is most applicable to a given enterprise.**

Keywords-component; Cloud Computing, Database, ERP, Linked Server, OLE DB, SQL

INTRODUCTION

When looking towards establishing or migrating to a cloud based Enterprise Resource Planning (ERP) system, specialists are challenged with providing seamless communication between the new and existing components. In many cases one of the existing components that will require seamless integration with the new cloud system is a database. Existing databases or legacy databases as this paper will from here refer to them may exist in varying capacities. An operational database may be present onsite and due to the specific requirements of the enterprise may be required to continue its service, interacting with the new cloud system. Alternatively the situation may arise that communication is required with an off-site database such as one belonging to a supplier or logistics partner.

In the linked database approach databases are configured to interact with each other almost seamlessly. Several common methods of establishing Linked Server communications exist but for the purpose of this paper discussion will revolve around the most common, this being OLE DB. Servers or systems that require data from another source are considered to consume the OLE DB interface while those servers vending said data are considered to provide the OLE DB interface [1]. Any database server that is required to allow access from an external system must have an account present which is granted restricted privileges to only the data and services necessary for said account to perform its function. Each database server required to connect to another is configured with connection information and security details as defined on the data source. This configuration is normally saved under an alias that executing code can prepend to an object name in order to access the resource of a remote database (e.g. Select * From RemoteDatabase.RemoteTable).

ADVANTAGES OF USING LINKED DATABASES

A. Simplicity

This approach can be considered clean, tidy and maintainable from a software engineering standpoint. This is because the majority of current production quality database systems support linked databases either natively or via the additional install of client/provider tools.

Any work required to connect two or more databases by these means can be considered a configuration rather than a development. Secondly assuming the correct privileges are configured, this method allows databases to leverage any features available locally on the remote database. The design of OLE DB can be credited for this as the goal of its development was to provide a standard interface to a large array of data sources. It achieves this by providing an abstracted view of a sources data, known as Rowsets [2].

Even more compelling as an argument for the use of linked databases is when cross-database queries are considered. This is the process of one SQL based database including objects belonging to another in a query. Using the linked databases of a cloud based ERP and that of a logistic partner as an example, it would be possible to report all orders that the enterprise has dispatched that are yet to of been successfully delivered.

B. Performance

Using Linked Servers it is possible to run extensive queries with each resulting record being constructed with data pulled from an array of databases. Without native linking between SQL based systems a service based transaction would need to be implemented. With large queries every data item that is required from a foreign server would require a request message to be generated and transmitted to the remote server. A handler application would then need to parse the request message, generate and execute the desired query before building a response message and delivering it back to the requesting server. The requesting server would subsequently be required to parse the response and merge the resulting data item into the result set.

OLE DB is able to perform distributed transactions efficiently because of the addition of the Distributed Transaction Coordinator (MSDTC). This service uses a specific phased protocol that ensures the outcome of any transaction is uniform across all involved systems [3]. It is due to the fact that this technology is so closely integrated with OLE DB that it is able to perform quickly and efficiently as little overhead is present due to a lack of generic design.

C. Reactivity

When a query is executed that includes data gained from a remote source via an OLE DB powered Linked Server it can, dependent on the system design, be considered current. This is due to the fact that during execution the query source acts as a consumer, contacting the data sources provider and requesting appropriate data entries. It can be assumed that because said data is direct from the source it is either current or in a state that the providing database design wishes any consumers to understand as current.

The "freshness" of data returned from remote databases via this method allows system integrators the ability to propagate data throughout the system in the knowledge that it is good to be utilized for mission critical decision making.

DISADVANTAGES OF USING LINKED DATABASES

A. Compatibility and Futureproofing

While the linked database approach seems advantageous there are drawbacks that need to be considered. Firstly how competently any given database can connect with another is dependent on the type, vendor and version. Major platforms such as SQL Server and Oracle Database Server support OLE DB however the same cannot be said of emerging data storage technologies. As a result of this interaction between SQL based systems and other types such as NOSQL based systems like Cassandra is not possible via Linked Server techniques.

This currently does not pose major problems for enterprise or systems integrators as the majority of database systems used in enterprise are SQL based and therefore for the most part OLE DB compatible. Given that the business and technological landscape is ever evolving and changing enterprise will inevitably need to react and change itself. It is highly likely that as a part of these changes an enterprise's ERP systems will require some modifying or extending. There are many scenarios that system integrators may encounter

where the existing all SQL databases are required to interface with NOSQL or alterative database systems. These scenarios could include the introduction of a new subsystem that includes and can only include an incompatible database type. Additionally a business merger or acquisition could lead to the requirement for merging two or more ERP systems that may include database types that are not appropriate for Linked Server use.

In instances such as these alternative means of transporting or querying data will need to be established. This method could consist of a web service whose purpose it is to provide an interface to the incompatible database's data. On a technical level this method would work however would lead to inconsistencies in design and methodology across the ERP system. Those data items that are communicated via linked databases would be up-to-date because as soon as a data item is inserted into its host database it will be visible to any queries run on servers linked to its host as discussed earlier in this paper. Data on a non-Linked Server would not be available until it had been replicated across via the implemented means to the existing system. The danger here is that important information imported from these new incompatible systems will always have a delay be it large or minor, before the ERP system as a whole is "aware" of it. This is because an OLE DB aware database cannot run cross database queries including itself and a none OLE DB aware system. This is a very real issue that integrators will need to consider as current trends have seen a big increase in demand for NOSQL based systems due to the scalability and performance properties they can offer [4].

The inconsistency and potential delays in propagating current data throughout the system could have significant impact on the enterprises business activities. Consider for instance that the overarching ERP system believes that a high throughput item is in significant stock. In reality it may be the case that the item is close to, or completely sold or used. The business may find that because of the delay in data being published through to the required location new stock is not requested in a timely enough fashion that disruption occurs in the businesses trading or operational activities.

B. Security Compromisation

In order to facilitate Linked Servers certain networking policy configurations need to be applied. This could be considered acceptable when an entire EPP system runs internally however when interfacing with an off-site or cloud based system opening the required ports will not be desirable. Having a database directly publicly accessible is not considered good practice as this limits the protection the local network security can provide.

Additionally given the volume of systems that are integrated via OLE DB powered linked servers a well-documented knowledge exists around its security weaknesses and means of exploiting them. One of the key areas open to exploitation is OLE DB's error reporting system. This can be used combined with SQL injection techniques by unauthorized entities in order to discover and potentially abuse areas of the database [5]. With considered design and security application it should be possible to raise the barrier to such attacks fairly highly making it to some extent a moot point. However a significant risk is present if the security strategy is not realized to its fullest.

C. Failiure Implications

Strong stability and uptime performance are characteristics that go towards defining an ideal ERP system [6]. Should such a system incorporate linked databases the increase in risk to stability and uptime should be considered.

Simply because the system relies on linked databases does not inherently mean it is any less fault tolerant, however it does open the door to ill-considered design ideas that can make it so. In terms of integration design a tradeoff is required with linked databases. This is due to the fact that the quicker the enterprise needs access to low level data and the broader they require that information to be the level of fault tolerance in this system needs to be compromised.

Consider the example of a management report that is generated on the fly from several linked database sources. If an issue exists with one of the databases or the link that binds it to the others has failed the whole report and anything that relies on it becomes unavailable. The consequences for the ERP system as a whole could in this instance be significant if it has not been designed in a fault tolerant manner which is difficult to do using Linked Server as systems tend to rely heavily on other systems in order to function.

to integrate via other means in the future is to occur. If in the short to medium term it is considered unlikely, opting for the simplest option of continuing the use of Linked Servers seems the natural choice. However, in the circumstance that this option is recommended it should also be stated that opting for a complete tried and trusted solution such as this would lead to a significant project in the future should the need arise to integrate via other means. Any Negatives associated with this option such as security or failure concerns can be minimized with intelligent design decisions.

Should an enterprise be in a position where a mixture of both Linked Server and other means of database integration are present it is most likely advisable to forfeit simplicity for consistency. In this instance a common, abstracted means of allowing any consuming element of the system to call for data from a providing part should be implemented. This is a costly approach as it will require the development of custom middleware however it does place the enterprise into an agile position moving forwards.

Taking it as a given that SQL based technologies have a limited lifespan as the demands for highly scalable and flexible alternative solutions increases. It should be accepted that at some point a change from SQL based and thus Linked Server compatible systems to an alternative solution is inevitable in some capacity be it whole or partial. The question systems integrators and enterprise need consider is whether to commit to the tried and tested Linked Server model and accept a large cost at some point in the future or implement a future system today and accept the risk that they may be buying in to a concept too early and while they may see the benefit in the short or medium term an expensive redevelopment on the horizon may exist.

CONCLUSION

It is evident that there are both advantages and disadvantages regarding propagating data throughout an ERP system via the method of OLE DB based Linked Servers. When considering its use system integrators need to consider the advantages and disadvantages in relation to not only where the enterprise is now as an entity but where it could potentially be in the future. With this in mind it is possible to make a number of high level, scenario based recommendations as to what circumstances the use of Linked Servers may or may not be appropriate.

In the instance where an enterprise's current systems utilise Linked Servers it needs to be considered how likely the need

REFERENCES

[1] A. Blackeley, J., "OLE DB: a component DBMS architecture," Data Engineering, 1996. Proceedings of the Twelfth International Conference on , vol., no., pp.203-204, 26 Feb-1 Mar 1996

[2] A. Blackeley, J., "Universal data access with OLE DB," Compcon '97. Proceedings, IEEE, vol., no., pp.2-7, 23-26 Feb 1997

[3] Limprecht, R., "Microsoft Transaction Server," Compcon '97. Proceedings, IEEE , vol., no., pp.14-18, 23-26 Feb 1997

[4] R. Padhy. P, M. Patra, R., S. Sarapathy. C. "RDBMS to NoSQL: Reviewing Some Next-Generation Non-Relational Databases" International Journal of Advanced Engineering Sciences and Tehnologies, Vol., No., pp. 11-1, 15-30 2011

[5] King, S., "Applying application security standards – a case study", Computers & Security, Vol.23, no.1, pp.17-21, Jan 2004

[6] Krasner, H.; , "Ensuring e-business success by learning from ERP failures," IT Professional , vol.2, no.1, pp.22-27, Jan/Feb 2000

Critical Failure Factors of ERP Implementation

Tan Ping Yee

School of Computing and Mathematics

University of Derby

Derby, United Kingdom

100241087@unimail.derby.ac.uk

Abstract—**With technological advances, Enterprise Resource Planning (ERP) has become increasingly important for enterprise to survive in the business environment. However, implementation of these systems is complex and costly. Most of the ERP implementations fail because project management did not manage the project well. This article identifies the critical failure factor in managing cloud projects during the implementation of ERP system. Differentiation of managing projects in cloud based ERP and traditional ERP systems identified and discussed. Key factors that cause failure in both traditional and cloud based ERP system also were examined and discussed.**

Keywords-critical failure factor; project management; cloud computing; ERP

INTRODUCTION

Enterprise Resource Planning (ERP) system are integrated software solutions that integrate all business functions such as human resources, production, sales and others by using single repository. With technological advances, ERP has become gradually more important for enterprises to survive in the business environment. Organisations with successful ERP implementation consider the ERP system as one of the most important innovations because they provide tangible and intangible benefits such as cost, customer lead times and production time reduction. However, implementing an ERP system is complex and expensive which can lead to failure.

It is not easy to judge whether a project has 'failed'. However, a project tends to be successful if it meets the three high-level criteria that are usually used by management. These three criteria are that the project should:

1. Deliver on time

2. Deliver within budget

3. Deliver the expected benefits.

Therefore, project failure can be defined as being a project that is late, over-budget and does not deliver expected functionality.

BACKGROUND

A. Project Management in ERP Implementation

"The project manager (PM) is the individual who acts as a leader to communicate and manage a clear vision of the goals, and manages the process so that that appropriate timing, resources and sequencing tasks produce agreed-on deliverables within scope and budget. Credibility is the most essential quality a PM must strive to acquire. More than just possessing technical knowledge of the software being implemented, the PM must have good business knowledge so the clients feel their needs and requirements are understood. Moreover, the PM must stay calm under stressful conditions and be able to make rapid and effective decisions in complex situations. He must be flexible and imaginative. Change is inevitable, and the PM must recognize the inherent discovery process in the project and control it, not stop it."[5]

From the above statement, the role of project manager can be identified as crucial in the ERP implementation. The project manager acts as a leader to communication, manages goals and objectives clearly, implement time and cost management, has a good knowledge about current technology and software and also business. Additionally, a project manager must have the ability to solve complex situations and must be flexible and also identify the intrinsic discovery process during the project and control it without stopping it.

Information Technology (IT) Managers identified that 77% of IT-related projects included in ERP implementation fails due to the primary reason of poor management and planning [6]. The scope, size and complexity of an ERP implementation are normally staggered by managers which will lead the management not initiating the essential level of detailed project management planning and control. Besides that, managing an ERP system implementation is tricky. Unanticipated events will arise that may increase the overall cost of the project. Therefore, it is crucial to understand the organisational structure and management. [2]

Due to the complexity of ERP systems, a project manager requires the ability of involvement in documentation and leadership which is important to control and manage the project activities, responsibilities and deadlines. With the appropriate documentation, it can help the manager to ensure the deadline and tasks are not missed. As a result, the project manager plays an important role in the process of developing and implementing a successful ERP system. [11] To drive success in the project management, adequate responsibility should be given to an individual or group of people. [10]

According to research of Wong, Scarbrough, Chau & Davison, four case studies have been evaluated. In the research, the main factor that causes ERP implementation is the poor planning, leading, managing and monitoring the project by project manager. [12] All of the projects from the four case studies could not accomplish effective project management of ERP implementation due to the lack of ERP knowledge, capability and poor project management skill.

KEY FACTORS IN ERP IMPLEMENTATION

A. Vendor Lock-In

Vendor lock-in is an important issue to be concerned by project manager. When vendor lock-in happened, the training and processes might be problematic to the users and organization because the information is inaccessible in a different branded format [4]. It is not easy to transfer from old version to newer version. Upgrading to newer version requires re-implementing customizations, time-consuming when doing retesting, and required costly additional hardware and infrastructure. As a result, organisations are unable to install a newer version of ERP system across their company completely due to the lock by provider.

Moreover, a massive obstacle faced by the users in implementing cloud is they have no control in the cloud-based services when it comes to frequent changes. One of the examples that happened in real life is the cloud service provider Coghead shut down which leads to putting their customer in serious trouble. Users who facing vendor lock-in need to rewrite their application in order to operate in another platform [4]. It not only will affect their business, but also their supplier and customer and also will faces huge losses during rewrite application time.

In order to prevent the occurrence of these problems, vendor lock-in must be avoided by project manager. One of the solutions is using standardized programming interface. A standardized programming interface allows cloud-based ERP system to move the system to a new cloud-based system easily. By using standardization, a variety of choices in cloud without vendor lock-in can be chosen by users as it can increase and accelerate the adoption of cloud computing [8]. By using more than one cloud services provider, user can have a backup for their system. Besides that, users have the opportunities to choose and use more than one service providers to perform different functions based on the criteria. Furthermore, standardization has the ability to reuse the existing data center resources which can help an organization to reduce the implementation time and cost.

B. Vendor and Software Selection

Vendors who have experience and knowledge in specific industries about certain application modules can help organisations to determine which suite will work best for them. [10] Therefore, it is vital when choosing a vendor. Questions about the vendor such as are their strategically aligned or concerning their vision for the future should be asked by project manager and he/she must consider the software provided by the vendor to make sure all the software are available. [3]

Software selection is crucial when managing an ERP project. One of the main challenges that an organisation faces is whether the software fits all their requirements. Project manager should seek for help through knowledgeable outsourcing if the organisation lacks knowledge of ERP systems. Successful ERP implementation can be increased if the organisations have analyzed their software and individual module needs. [6]

C. Implementation Cost

Project cost planning in ERP implementation is crucial because one of the reasons projects fail is over budget. The project manager can choose either insourcing or outsourcing or both. Purchasing prewritten software is always cheaper compared to in-house development; however the costs of implementation would increase by three to five times that of the purchase price if the degree of customization increases. It could exceed 30% of the overall budget when hiring consultants if it takes longer time for implementation. Besides that, the upfront costs for purchasing IT infrastructure are very high. Additionally, IT personnel should be hired to ensure the implementation is successful. Therefore, project manager should ensure they have adequate budgets to purchase necessary resources before the implementation of an ERP system.

D. Implementation Time

The implementation of ERP system is time consuming because of its complexity. A typical ERP implementation normally takes 14 months' to complete. [3] There are four issues that will affect the implementation times, these are:

1. *The number of modules being implemented*
2. *The scope of the implementation (different functional units or across multiple units spread out globally)*
3. *The extent of customization*
4. *The number of interfaces with other application.[3]*

Therefore, they can identify that the greater number of issues above the longer time it will take to complete an ERP implementation.

E. User Training and Involvement

One of the significant factors of many ERP system failures is due to the inefficient training. Although millions of dollars and thousands of hours have been used during the ERP implementation projects, without the appropriate training, the project would still end in failure. [1] The main reason of training for ERP implementation is to increase the knowledge and expertise level of the employees and ensure that they are comfortable with the system. [2] *"Training is not only using the new system, but also in new processes and in understanding the integration within the system."* Therefore, training consultants should address all aspects of the system and transfer their internal knowledge to employees. [10] User training in ERP is demanding due to the complexity of the system. Training consultants are difficult to transfer their internal knowledge to the employees in a short period of time and the difficulty will increase if the users have computer phobia or lack of computing expertise. Thus, an organisation must enhance employee's skill and knowledge by providing appropriate training opportunities on a continuous basis to achieve the changing needs of the business and employees. [3]

F. IT Infrastructure

Technology planning such as choosing the most suitable IT infrastructure and networking is a critical success factor in an organisation. [2] IT must be considered before ERP implementation matters and how it may influence the business process. Organisations must invest in new technologies and also to stabilise the current technology and remove old systems to ensure the system can integrate the current business processes. [9] By using cloud, it would be easily managed by IT staff as new layers of complexity can be ignored because ERP is already a complex enterprise infrastructure. The existing management products including physical and virtual servers can be well-monitored with the management capabilities.

G. System Testing

One of the main reasons ERP implementation is inappropriate is when it is implemented without planned testing before going live. Testing an ERP system is crucial to ensure that the software can integrate with the business process and must confirm it can run properly. All the functionalities should be tested both alone and in combination with the current functionality. [1]

CONCLUSIONS

TABLE I.   COMPARISON OF FAILURE KEY FACTOR BETWEEN TRADITIONAL ERP AND CLOUD BASED ERP

Key Factors	Traditional ERP	Cloud Based ERP
Vendor and Software Selection	May need to choose multi-vendor to ensure all the software are available. Software should be chosen carefully to make sure it can fit into the system. Difficult to change to another vendor because the new ERP system may not support the current infrastructure.	All the software provided by Cloud supplier. However, software must be chosen carefully to ensure can fit into the system. Project manager should choose open standard Cloud provider to prevent vendor lock-in. ERP system should be installed in more than one cloud provider as a back-up.
Implementation Cost	Requires large upfront and ongoing investments to purchase and manage the software, servers, and facilities necessary to run it.	Initial costs are typically much lower because can simply implement the software to user requirements and then access it through user computer's internet connection.
Implementation Time	Much longer than cloud ERP implementation.	Shorter than traditional ERP implementation

Key Factors	Traditional ERP	Cloud Based ERP
	Normally takes 14 months to complete the implementation.	because all the software, hardware, IT infrastructure are provided by the cloud supplier. Usually takes 3-6 months
User training and involvement	Requires more IT personnel to install, maintain and run the system. User training is important to ensure the user can handle the system.	Requires less IT personnel that to install, maintain and run the system. However, user training still is a must to ensure they will be able to handle the system.
IT infrastructure	Organisation required to buy and upgrade their own IT infrastructure	IT infrastructure provided by the cloud and continues upgrading
Testing	No matter whether using the traditional or cloud based ERP system, testing must always must be done before going live. Testing is important to ensure the software works successfully and the user can handle it and business processes are practical.	

Table 1 shows that the comparison of key factors between traditional and cloud-based ERP system which will cause the implementation fails. Although the cloud based ERP system is better than traditional ERP system in terms of vendor and software selection, implementation cost and time, IT infrastructure and more. Nevertheless the project management of the cloud based ERP system is still vital. Without proper planning, an ERP implementation will never be successful. Besides this, project manager must consider testing as an important factor. With appropriate training, not only ensures the user can handle the system and business processes well, it can also increase the success rate of ERP implementation.

REFERENCES

[1]   Al-Mashari, Al-Mudimigh and Zairi. (2003) *Enterprise Resource Planning: A taxonomy of Critcal Factors.* European Journal of Operational Research. 146(2) pp.352-364.

[2]   Bhatti, T. R. (2005) *Critical Success Factors for the Implementation of Enterprise Resource Planning (ERP): Empirical Validation*, the second International Conference on Innovation in Information Technology, pp. 1-10.

[3]   Bingi, Sharna abd Godla. (1999) *Critical Issues Affecting an ERP Implementation.* Information System Management, 16(3) pp. 7-14.

[4]   Chow, et al (2009) *Controlling Data in the Cloud: Outsoursing Computation Without Outsourcing Control.* Proceedings of 2005 ACM workshop on Cloud Computing Security, *pp. 85-90.*

[5]   Mousseau, P. (1998) *ERP project call for multi-talented managers.* Computing Canada. 24(42) pp.30.

[6]   Muscatello, J & Chen, I. J. (2008*) Enterprise Resource Planning (ERP) Implementations: Theory and Practice.* International Journal of Enterprise Information Systems, 4(1) pp.63-83.

[7]   Noudoostbeni, A., Ismail, N. A., Jenatabadi, H. S. & Yasin, N. M. (2010) An Effective End-User Knowledge Concern Training Method in Enterprise Resource Planning (ERP) Based on Critical Factors (CFs) in Malaysia SMEs. International Journal of Business and Management 5(7) pp. 63 – 76.

[8]   Parameswaran, A. V. & Chaddha A (2009) *Cloud Interoperability and Standardization.*SETLabs Briefings, 7(7).

[9]   Shirouyehzad, Dabestani and Badakhshian (2011) *The FMEA Approach to Identification of Critical Failure Factors in ERP*

Implementation. Journal of International Business Research. 4(3) pp.254-263.

[10] Shou, Y. & Ying, Y. (2005) *Critical Failure Factors of Information System Projects in Chinese Enterprises*. Proceedings of ICSSSM '05. 2 pp.823-827.

[11] Snider, Silveira and Balakrishnan (2009) *ERP implementation at SMEs: analysis of five Canadian cases*. International Journal of Operation & Production Management, 29(1) pp.4-29.

[12] Wong, Scarbrough, Chau & Davison (2005) *Critical Failure Factors in ERP Implementation*. PACIS 2005 pp. 492-505.

Strategies for Managing the Integration of Complex Legacy Systems

Richard Matthew Bowbanks

School of Computing and Mathematics,
University of Derby, U.K
rmbow@hotmail.co.uk

Abstract— **This document specifies the strategic problems when integrating the legacy systems of an organisation and methods to overcome such problems both in a behavioral manner as well as at a technical level.**

Keywords – systems integration; legacy; strategy

INTRODUCTION

Reference [1] defines an enterprise resource planning (ERP) system as a system that assists the pursuit of organisational objectives using a set of integrated programs, fulfilling a need to share data across many departments, reduce future costs and establish the management of business processes.

This article considers the strategies that an enterprise might adopt to overcome the challenges present when integrating existing systems both at a technical level and human resource management level. We shall begin by identifying the problems present at an organizational level, before scrutinizing various strategies that organisations adopt. The article concludes by identify the effective strategies for integrating complex legacy systems.

STRATEGIC PROBLEM AREAS

A. Resistance Occuring from the Workforce

Reference [1] suggests two sources of resistance from users during new technology adoption. The first is an employee's adverse perception of the risk as a result of a decision to adopt the new technology. The second is habitual change in that users become comfortable with repeated daily tasks. Any disruption to these tasks can be de-motivating for the immediate future. Furthermore, organization must be able to respond to internal customer demands in order to avoid long term difficulties [1].

The adoption of a service culture is a contributor to workforce resilience. The adoption of cloud architectures requires service thinking, hence can too result in high levels of resistance. A case study of Rolls Royce demonstrates that the functionality of new systems may not be fully appreciated, due to changes in the organisational culture as a result of integrating different departments [8].

B. Dirty Data

Dirty data is an error or inconsistency in the data as a byproduct from a company's legacy systems [7]. Dirty data can result in difficulties when implementing integration strategies of new ERP systems, and therefore carry high costs that can make implementation procedures difficult to justify [7].

C. Integration and Customisation Issues

Reference [6] argues that it is integration of ERP into an organisation's existing systems that is the single biggest contributor to system failure, accounting for nearly 82%. Integration of the various systems is difficult due to the number of separate systems that need integrating; however ERP systems do offer a partial solution [6].

ERP packages do not allow for sufficient customisation and therefore cannot often be tailored to business needs [6]. Reference [6] provides a survey which states in a sample of sixty-seven, that ¾ suffered customisation issues both during implementation as well as after. Reference [6] goes onto state that it is better to match ERP systems to the organisation rather than attempting to customize the software.

CASE STUDY – ROLLS ROYCE

A. Business Background

Rolls Royce previously had 1500 systems in place which resulted in high costs, poor maintenance and data inconsistencies. The DBMS's in place made it difficult for the individual systems to interface with one another so Rolls Royce outsourced a team management specialists and SAP consultants. An internal team consisting of top management and experts of the legacy systems were also used [8].

B. Implementation Strategy

When implementing the new system (SAP R/3), Rolls Royce found that their complex business structure made it difficult for the software to satisfy the business needs. Therefore, the business processes were changed to meet the requirements of the software. To change the software would have resulted in costs making completion of the project impossible [8].

Rolls Royce also found that their existing data was not compatible with the new system software and so was not transferable. To overcome this problem, Rolls Royce ran their existing system and the ERP system alongside one another until the existing system was out phased completely [8].

CHANGE MANAGEMENT STRATEGIES

References [1] and [3] propose a framework for addressing three factors of user resistance to change. These include system awareness response, feelings response and adoption intention response.

A. Awareness Response

References [1] and [3] identify a communication strategy which involves identifying the benefits of the new system to other members of the workforce as well as operational features. Most ERP implementation projects fail due to poor communication; however well formed communication strategies improve awareness response from employees [1].

B. Feelings Response

In order to improve workers feelings, the organisation should adopt cost minimization strategies, as well as involve employees both individually and in groups in the completion of the project [1]. Training should be frequent and in depth [3]. Reference [1] argues that the quality of user interfaces as part of the new system should be maximized and illustrates the three stages of overcoming resistance to change on behalf of workers.

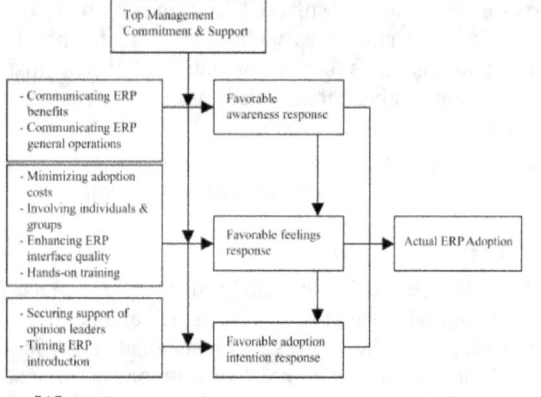

[1]

Figure 1. Overcoming resistence for ERP adoption

C. Adoption Intention Response

In order to improve adoption intent, the organization should gain support from more influential groups and leaders. By doing so will discourage individuals from developing rebellious attitudes [1]. Reference [1] goes onto state that systems should be introduced once worker

resilience has been overcome to obtain the desired effects. Reference [3] proposes the use of a project champion to improve intention response of employees.

D. Status Evaluation Phase

Monitoring and evaluating the strategies is the final phase for top management. It is vital that there are some measurements of performance in place to assess whether the required outcome was obtained and to provide management with feedback. Reference [1] states that the feedback received should be timely, accurate and systematic.

ENTERPRISE APPLICATION INTEGRATION

Enterprise Application Integration (EAI) has led to confusion amongst writers [2]. Reference [2] states that EAI has been limited to integrating ERP systems to other ERP systems. The use of EAI enables the integration of all other applications in the organization [2].

EAI is used to coordinate all of the computing resources in an enterprise using its existing systems whilst sill enabling the adoption of new applications [5]. EAI is particularly useful to organisations wishing to integrate their legacy systems because it avoids the need to engage in complex programming [5]. This in turn saves large amounts of time as well as expense for the company. Rather, it uses specialist middleware to form a bridge between various applications [5].

A. Critical Success Factors of EAI

Reference [4] identifies critical success factors of EAI for the implementation of new systems. These include not using a single EAI service to overcome all of the organisation's problems, providing adequate training for the work force, understanding the cost and budgeting constraints for the project and overcoming resistance to change from employees. We have already evaluated change management in overcoming resistance to change which highlighted frequent and in depth training as part of a favorable feelings response. Understanding costs and budget restraints requires effective financial management and continuous monitoring.

B. EAI &ERP

Reference [5] contrasts the use of Enterprise Resource Planning (ERP) in relation to EAI and the impact either can have both on the organization as well as the project. The fundamental areas looked at are that ERP is more likely to bring about staff resilience than EAI because the organization is required to re-model its internal processes (BPR) which results in uncertainty amongst staff as to their new roles. Reference [5] goes onto state that ERP takes longer to implement than EAI, and ERP is typically supported in centralized organizational structures whereby business decisions are made from higher authorities and activities are delegated downwards to the lower levels.

[5]

TABLE VII.   TECHNICAL & BEHAVIOURAL FACTORS

		ERP	EAI
Technical	Degree of BPR	High/Medium	Medium/Low
	Integration Method	Process Integration	Process Mapping
	Implementation Period	Long	Medium
Behavioral	Degree of Resistance	High	Low
	Business Process	Centralized	Decentralized
	Internalization Period	Long	Short

EAI is best used in organizations operating a decentralized structure which supports more of a team environment. Reference [5] goes onto state that that ERP takes longer for an individual to adopt and become familiar with, which can be another reason for a higher level of resistance whereas EAI is said to take a shorter amount of time for an individual to accept. This shows that internalization and the degree of resistance are positively correlated.

CASE STUDY – EAI INTEGRATION PROCESS FOR FINANCIAL SERVICE PROVIDER

A. Business Problem

Reference [4] produces a case study for a financial institution (FI) which needed a newly integrated system due to customer demands for 'self-service' banking. The FI had previously operated using 20 back-end applications with interfaces built between the front and back-end of the application, otherwise known as a point-to-point integration approach. This resulted in a complex number of interfaces being used for its users.

B. Project Initiation & Requirments Specification

The approach started with a 3 month preliminary investigation of the organisational needs for EAI as well as employing a consultant. The FI developed an understanding of its business processes and how integrating its applications would aid in such processes using business process models.

C. Integration Architecture Analysis & EAI Evaluation

It was found that the new integrated approach would need to support the use of future banking channels such as mobile banking. Therefore, a common set of application interfaces (CAI) were created for back-end applications; and an integration hub would enable communication to take place between front-end applications and the CAI.

The criteria for selection of an EAI tool were fundamentally based on the flexibility of the EAI tool in relation to business processes, reliability in respect to server up-time; and ability to integrate new front-end applications in the future.

D. Development of CAI

Much of the functionality and design for the new system was taken from existing systems. This would ease some resistance from workers wanting to operate regular practices. Some new functionality was added to improve efficiency of business processes. The CAI was rolled out gradually over a period of time. Configuration and customization of the EAI tools took several months to complete due to the large volume of business processes already in place.

E. Phased Rollout

The first stage of the rollout phase involved installing the EAI tool in the FI's business environment to make it usable. The following stages involved integrating the front-end application which handled far fewer transactions. The EAI tool followed two months after and telephone and other channels followed soon after.

F. Technical & Behavioural Factors

From the details of the case, we can imitate the table supplied by [5] to evaluate the effectiveness of the EAI approach used.

TABLE VIII.   APPLICATION OF EAI TO CASE STUDY VI

		EAI
Technical	Degree of BPR	Medium
	Integration Method	
	Implementation Period	Medium/ Long
Behavioral	Degree of Resistance	Low
	Business Process	Decentralized
	Internalization Period	Short

There was little indication in the case of BPR other than an understanding of the business processes involved. The FI was able to easily tackle user resistance by including existing functionality, however there were indications that the new system needing to be rolled out over a period of 2 months.

G. Change Management Recommendations

It is important for the FI that the project has the support of influential leaders. This can be done by involving groups in the implementation process. This also provides an opportunity to communicate the benefits and operations of the system. A cost minimization strategy would gain a favorable response from the workforce and help maintain budget constraints.

CONCLUSION

When developing integration strategies, organisations need to consider not only how to integrate the firm's legacy systems but the impact that such change will have on other areas such as resilience from the workforce or inconsistencies in the existing data with the new system.

The two forms of strategy identified in this paper are change management and EAI, both of which are essential for integrating legacy systems. Change management strategies can typically overcome issues relating to staff resistance and changes to working practices, whereas EAI can avoid problems which may arise from firms adopting an ERP approach such as unnecessary changes to business processes as well as longer completion times.

REFERENCES

[1] Aladwani, A. (2001), Change management strategies for successful ERP implementation, *Business Process Managemen.*. Vol. 7 No. 3, pp. 266-275

[2] Irani, Z. Themistocleous, M. & Love, P. (2003), The impact of enterprise application integration on information systems lifecycles, *Information & Management*, Vol. 41, pp. 177-187

[3] Kemp, M.J. & Low, G.C. (2008), ERP innovation implmentation model incoporating change management, *Business Process Management Journal*, Vol. 14 No. 2, pp. 228-242

[4] Lam, W. (2005), Investigating success factors in enterprise application integration: a case-driven analysis, *European Journal of Information Systems*, Vol. 14, pp. 175-187

[5] Lee, J. Siau, K. & Hong, S. (2003), Enterprise Integration with ERP and EAI, Vol. 46 No. 2, pp.54-60

[6] Themistocleous, M. Irani, Z. O'Keefe, R. & Paul, R. (2001), ERP Problems and Application Integration Issues: An Empirical Survey, *Information Systems Evaluation Group*

[7] Vosburg, J. & Kumar, A. (2001), Managing dirty data in organizations using ERP: lessons from a case study, *Industrial Management & Data Systems,* Vol. 101 No. 1, pp. 21-31

[8] Yusuf, Y. Gunasekaran, A. & Abthorpe, M.S. (2004), Enterprise information systems project implementation: A case study of ERP in Rolls-Royce, *Production Economics*, Vol. 87, pp. 251-266

Legal aspects of cloud ERP

Saeed Alshawi (100239985)
School of Computing and Mathematics
University of Derby
Derby, UK
100239985@unimail.derby.co.uk

Over the years, various definitions and descriptions of cloud computing have emerged. To mention but a few, cloud computing has been said to involve the delivery of computing facilities as a service over the internet. It allows access to be shared while resources are located in different places, with the possibility that the platform is controlled by different entities. It can also be seen as a kind of utility model of computing where the user can buy computing capability as he needs it without the infrastructure cost of purchasing and implementing a system specifically for himself. Based on the foregoing definitions, the bottom line of cloud computing is that it refers to "internet-based computing".

INTRODUCTION

Cloud computing is very much the latest technology at the moment. This is because it has numerous benefits particularly when compared against legacy computing which involves the storage of data on a computer hard drive or a local server. The mere fact that cloud computing allows the storage of the data on the internet makes it more efficient than legacy computing in storing data. It has been argued that this model is preferable particularly for businesses with a high sales volume. As a benefit, cloud computing services are generally cheaper. It can also reduce energy consumption significantly and can save businesses the trouble of fixing and servicing IT installations.

However, cloud computing raises genuine legal concerns which are not unconnected with the fact that it is a relatively new technology. Its mode of operation also intensifies the legal problem. These concerns can be broadly summed as deriving from privacy, data protection and contractual issues and these concerns will be identified and analysed below. However, before highlighting them, a brief summary of the nature of cloud computing will be provided.

A. Summary of Cloud Computing

There are three main types of cloud computing services; 1) Infrastructure as a Service (IaaS), 2) Software as a Service (SaaS), and 3) Platform as a Service (PaaS)

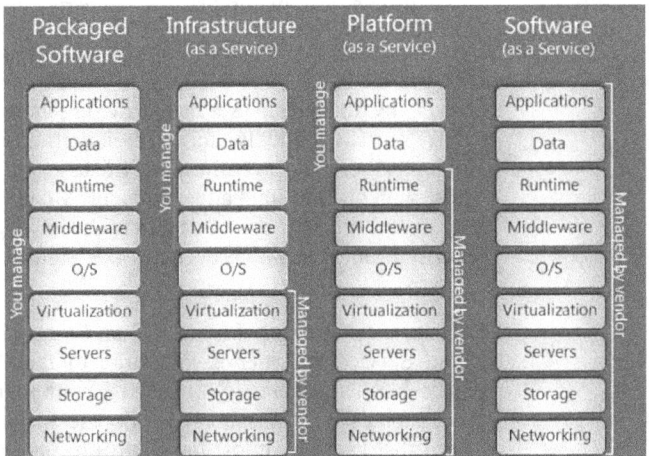

Firgure1. Main types of cloud computing

Regarding its reach and accessibility, cloud service could also be categorised as public, private or hybrid. A public cloud is hosted at the provider's premises while the infrastructure is shared by different customers. On the other hand, the infrastructure of a private cloud is dedicated to a particular customer, while hybrid cloud is a mixture of both.

B. Legal Aspects

The major concern with ERP cloud computing is the issue of privacy and data protection. First, considering that the service is undertaken in a truly global scale whereby data from one jurisdiction could be stored in a very remote location, issues would naturally arise when one has to determine which of the various legislations in the different jurisdictions apply. This naturally causes uncertainty as to where the data is transferred to and where and how the data should be retained. The enormity of this legal challenge can be appreciated further when it concerns very sensitive institutions such as financial and health institutions. The fact that one does not know who the document is accessed by or where it is stored could potentially fracture the growth of cloud computing. However, the seriousness of the concern will depend largely on whether the organisation involved buys into a private cloud or a public cloud.

a) Privacy

The risk will be higher in a public cloud but that does not mean that the private cloud is insulated from the privacy concerns. For instance, while privacy concerns can be mitigated through anonymised and pseudonymised data, encrypted data, and sharding or fragmentation of data, the privacy risk will still exist where the customer omits or deletes obvious direct identifiers such as names, while leaving indirect identifiers untouched. In such cases, the protective measures will not be enough to render information non-personal.

Privacy issues are also major challenges in the Cloud Computing, which includes protection of identity information, transaction histories and sensitive data. The idea of Cloud Computing is to transfer the computing load to the shared infrastructure. Such idea will cause the problem that customers' private information faces the risk of unauthorized access and retrieval. We will discuss the major privacy concerns in the following:

- Unauthorized secondary usage: Users' data can be utilized by the Cloud Service Provider in some cases, most commonly form is advertisement. However, there are several usage of data is against users' will, such as junk advertisement. Moreover, such unauthorized usage of data may cause serious security problems, which becomes one significant concern.

- Lack of user control: In the Cloud Computing, Cloud Service Provider is in charge of the data procession. So there is a case that the data procession is not transparent to the users, which means that users have lost the control of the data. Such case raises the concern about the theft and misuse of users' data. Moreover, users' privacy can be easily uncovered. So there is need to establish the privacy protection mechanism to deal with this.

- Unclear responsibility: There is one problem related to the privacy that it is sometimes unclear about which Cloud Service Provider is responsible for privacy protection, detecting who use and modify the user data or ensuring user data privacy requirements. Users are also concerned about whether the rights of data procession of one single third party can be transferred to another third party if bankruptcy is emerged.

Data Ownership and Data Location

Another concern relates to the question of ownership of the cloud. It has been contended that a service provider should not be allowed to breach the ownership right of customers merely because the identity of the customer is protected. In other words, protection is as much a question of ownership as it is of privacy.

Cloud Computing offers freedom access of information. Clients do not always have an idea of where is the information located? In general, this is not a matter in customer point of view. For instance, pictures add to Facebook account and emails messages can be located in anywhere in the world and Facebook members are normally not worried. Still, this is a

different story when it is become for a sensitive information for an enterprise which the use cloud-based services, for sure the enterprise wants to know the location of their information. They may also need specific. (e.g. the data have to within EU).

An agreed contract, amongst the customer and the service provider and the customer that where the information must be or exist in on a specified server. The concern is customers are, occasionally, not conscious of the suggestion of major points in the contract is agreed in advance. Even though, cloud providers should be in charge to guarantee the systems security (which include the information) and deliver strong verification to protect clients' data, all the time, what is essential is that the cloud service providers not only notify customers, but also provide the required info that the customer do not know about. UK laws are an example with respect to data privacy. The law essential private data of UK residents must locate within UK. The Cloud service provider responsibility; knows this and counsels customers for that reason. If the customers recognize it then clearly the customer can recommend, even request, that the data be kept on a device that physically locate in UK; Legal requirements in many other countries deferent than the UK one regarding location and movement of personal data. The movement of data from one location to another is another issue. Data is primarily kept at a proper location choose by the Cloud provider. However, it is regularly moved from one location to another. Cloud providers have agreements with each other and they use each other's resources. Customers do not always know this and commonly it does not matter.

BUSINESSES CONCERNS

Issues are also likely to arise regarding regulatory compliance. This could raise a lot of concerns for businesses. For instance the European Database Directive provides that the data controller has to comply with data protection legal obligations including any requirement to register with the relevant national authority before processing personal data. A company might find itself in a dilemma in ascertaining whether the data controller is within Europe.

In addition, a unique problem that could also arise is that the present laws in the different jurisdictions might adequately deal with the problems. For example, the concept of "controller" and "processor" in the Database Directive leads cannot be rationally transposed to the cloud computing. This is because, while the Directive envisaged the controller to be the provider or vendor, it is actually the customer that is the controller in cloud computing.

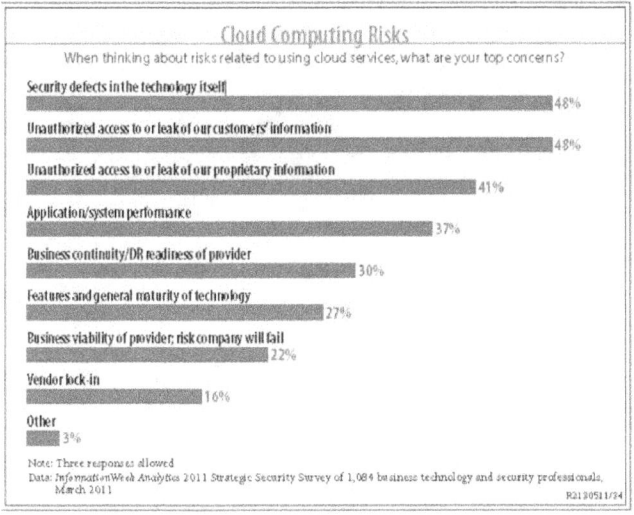

Firgure2. Cloud Computing Risks

CONCLUSION

The potential legal pitfalls of cloud computing have been identified. However, it should be noted that it is not all doom and gloom as there are signs that the authorities are ready to rise up to the challenge. For instance, Europe is proposing a new Directive which perhaps would address the shortcomings of the present Directive. A noteworthy provision in the proposed Directive is about the "right to be forgotten". This law might be crucial where a customer ends a contractual relationship with the service provider and wants to ensure that it data are wiped off the provider's site.

Regarding the uncertainty surrounding the privacy issue, it has been suggested that customers should look beyond governmental regulation by arming themselves with the avenues in contract. They could for example, enter into a contractual agreement with the cloud provider with the condition that the cloud provider will only process personal data in accordance with the data controller's instruction. The provider can also be made to commit to taking necessary measures in order to secure personal data.

Having noted the recommendation in the preceding paragraph, care must be taken so that we do not go into overdrive in our effort to secure personal data. That is why it is contended that so as not to compromise the growth of the booming technology; the recommendation made by Hon et al should be taken seriously. They have suggested that not all data stored with the service provider should be considered personal data. For instance, where a data is fully encrypted, it should not be considered as personal data. The practical effect will be that the service provider will be able to store the data in another jurisdiction without infringing the privacy and data protection provisions.

REFERENCES

Books

[1] Rowland D, Kohl U, Charlesworth A. (2012) Information Technology Law. 4th ed. London: Routledge, pp 430.

[2] Reed C. (2011). Computer Law. 7th ed. Oxford: Oxford University Press, pp 55-56.

Articles

[3] Hon W, Hörnle J, and Millard C. (2011). "The Problem of 'Personal Data' in Cloud Computing - What Information is Regulated? The Cloud of Unknowing, Part 1" Queen Mary University of London, School of Law Legal Studies Research Paper No. 75/2011, pp. 5.

[4] Metri P, Sarote G (2011). "Privacy Issues and Challenges in Cloud Computing"

[5] International Journal of Advanced Engineering Sciences and Technologies Vol. 5, No. 1, 001 – 006.

[6] Reed C, Mell P, and Grance T. (2009). "The NIST Definition of Cloud Computing version 15" US National Institute of Standards and Technology; Reed 56-57.

[7] Reed C (2010) "Information "Ownership" in the Cloud Queen Mary University of London, School of Law Legal Studies Research Paper No. 45/2010;.

[8] Ohm P (2010) "Broken Promises of Privacy: responding to the surprising failure of anonymization" http://papers.ssrn.com/sol3/papers.cfm?abstract_id=1450006.

[9] Nicole Ozer N, and Conley C (2010). "Cloud Computing: Storm Warning for Privacy" ACLU of Northern California.

[10] Hon W, Hörnle J, and Millard C. (2011). "Data Protection Jurisdiction and Cloud Computing – When are Cloud Users and Providers Subject to EU Data Protection Law? The Cloud of Unknowing, Part 3" Queen Mary University of London, School of Law Legal Studies Research Paper No 84/2011.)

[11] J. Clerk Maxwell, A Treatise on Electricity and Magnetism, 3rd ed., vol. 2. Oxford: Clarendon, 1892, pp.68–73.

[12] I. S. Jacobs and C. P. Bean, "Fine particles, thin films and exchange anisotropy," in Magnetism, vol. III, G. T. Rado and H. Suhl, Eds. New York: Academic, 1963, pp. 271–350.

[13] K. Elissa, "Title of paper if known," unpublished.

[14] R. Nicole, "Title of paper with only first word capitalized," J. Name Stand. Abbrev., in press.

[15] Y. Yorozu, M. Hirano, K. Oka, and Y. Tagawa, "Electron spectroscopy studies on magneto-optical media and plastic substrate interface," IEEE Transl. J. Magn. Japan, vol. 2, pp. 740–741, August 1987 [Digests 9th Annual Conf. Magnetics Japan, p. 301, 1982].

[16] M. Young, The Technical Writer's Handbook. Mill Valley, CA: University Science, 1989.

Key Security Concerns with Cloud ERP Systems

Thomas Peet

School of Computing and Mathematics
University of Derby
Derby, UK
t.peet2@unimail.derby.ac.uk

Cloud computing is the latest trend in modern computing and cloud based ERP systems are one of areas that are benefiting from this new technology. However organizations must look at the key security issues that come with cloud based ERP systems and how to ensure that the vendor is complying with the key security concerns that surround it.

Keywords-component; Security; Cloud computing; ERP; Data Security; SaaS;

INTRODUCTION

Traditionally ERP systems were stored centrally on a companies sever and accessed from within the companies network by the employees. In modern times cloud computing is being heavily adopted in industry. While Cloud computing offers many benefits for communication: the availability of a wide range of software applications, vast amounts of (if not unlimited) storage and high processing power all in a low cost solution. Security has been one of the leading factors in organizations being reluctant to take on cloud computing and Software as a Service (SaaS).

As with any on-site ERP solution there are many areas of security that need to be address within cloud ERP systems. They key areas being physical security, transmission security, data security and application security [1].

PHYSICAL SECURITY

Contrary to its name, data and applications in the cloud are not situated in the sky; rather they are stored in data center somewhere in the world, usually the location is unknown to the organization. This section looks at the physical security of the data centers building, a physical security breach refers to somebody with malicious intent has physical access to the hardware where your organization's application is running or where the data is stored. A malicious attack on hardware may not cause data loss (as long as sufficient data security and fallbacks are in place) but it could cause serious downtime to you ERP system.

A. Personnel within the data center

High-level policies should be in place to govern and control who within the data center can see the data; only data administrators should be able to access the data. Access to hardware such as servers and data stores should be limited to only authorized personnel using modern security authentication such as ID cards, fingerprint or retina scans.

It is important to know what sorts of background checks have been completed on personnel that have access to you data. A company considering using a cloud based ERP service should check if the vendor is SAS 70 audited and if not ask if they should consider demanding that the vendor is SAS 70 audited [1].

B. External threats

Securing from external threats is vitally important and as any physical security breaches could offer a malicious user or a hacker access to very sensitive data. The SANS institute [2] has put together a document that outlines security protocols that data centers should follow in order to avoid a security breach. These include:

1) Site parimiter
There should be a high fence at least 20 feet from all sides of the building with guarded kiosks at every entry point. There should be no signs advertising that the building is a data center or the vendor.

2) Surveillance
There should be CCTV covering the entire building, car parks and neighboring property. All employees and visitors must park in the car parks and any car park otherwise should be towed.

3) Access points
Loading docks and all doors on the outside of the building should have automatic authentication Each entrance should have a security kiosk and physical barriers. All personell and equipment entering and leaving the facility should be logged.

TRANSMISSON SECURITY

The data for the ERP systems has to move between the clients, server and database because of this there is an opportunity for the data to be intercepted. To ensure the data cannot be viewed if intercepted the data needs to be encrypted. There are several different methods of encrypting the data including Secure Socket Layer (SSL), RSA, Data Encryption Standard (DES) and triple DES [1].

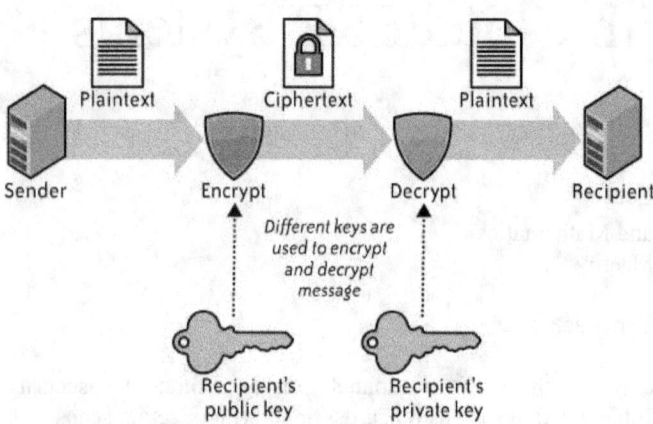

Figure 1. Data transmission encryption [3]

Due to ERP systems running on external clouds the data is sent over the Internet and in some cases over wireless networks cloud based ERP systems make use of SSL. SSL is supported by all browsers and uses security protocols such as HTTP and HTTPS. SOAP is another way Cloud ERP systems can encapsulate data and communicate securely between applications. SOAP uses XML to secure additional data allowing applications to communicate more efficiently than using HTTP.

DATA & STORAGE SECURITY

Data security is the most important factor in securing cloud based ERP systems as it limits access to data objects to specific individuals. Different levels of data security include read-only, edit, insert, and delete. Data security can be set at the application or object level [1].

Data security in cloud ERP applications is dealt in the same manor as self hosted applications; authenticated users are allowed access to parts of data based on roles assigned by the system. In a typical scenario, a sales person only access to information to clients that they handle so they cannot view client data that is not needed for them. The system can often help with this process by allowing administrators the ability to set roles to sets of users such as sales, accounting and delivery [4].

It is also important to know what protocols are in place in case data is lost due to hardware failure. All Cloud ERP vendors will have a backup policy, it is highly important that the client is fully aware of the vender's policy regarding backups, you should know who often backups are taken and how and where they are stored. Backups must be stored in facilities with the same high security standards as discussed previously in this paper [5].

APPLICATION SECUITY

When talking about application security we look at how cloud ERP systems handle User Authentication and how secure the application is in terms of software.

Not only is user authentication key for controlling access rights to users but also it is also key to logging what a user does in the system. If a user copies sensitive data onto an external device this could be logged on seen by the administrator. It is important that they system had a strong password criteria and that the passwords are changed frequently for example every couple of months [6].

CONCLUSION

When a company is looking to take advantage of Cloud based ERP systems it is important that they examine in-depth the security issues that they may face and how secure their data will be. The client must ask serious questions to the vendor before any decision is made. It is recommended that an audit is done on the vendor following the SAS 70 guidelines. One a decision is made the vender must make sure a good service level agreement is in place with the vendor so that these security expectations are not breached in the future.

The security issues are similar with cloud based and traditional ERP systems although there are some further concerns with cloud based ERP systems and cloud computing as a whole, if done correctly if can be much more secure that a self hosted solution. The data centers that the ERP venders use are often much safer than a companies self hosted server. The data centers have security in place that would not be cost effective to an organization to carry out themselves.

Security is the major factor holding companies back from converting to cloud based ERP however if care is taken and the vendor if complying to all the points made then the benefits to the client are great. They can save money on hardware, security procedures, management and much more.

REFERENCES

[1]   Johnson, D. (2011, October 6). *Security Issues in Cloud ERP*. Retrieved March 12, 2012, from ERP Cloud News: http://erpcloudnews.com/2011/10/security-issues-in-cloud-erp/

[2]   Heare, S. (2001). *Data Center Physical Security Checklist*. SANS Institute.

[3]   Mather, T., Kumaraswamy, S., & Latif, S. (2007). *Cloud Security and Privacy: An Enterprise Perspective on Risks and Compliance*. CA: O'Reilly Media.

[4]   Hofmann, P.; Woods, D.; , "Cloud Computing: The Limits of Public Clouds for Business Applications," *Internet Computing, IEEE* , vol.14, no.6, pp.90-93, Nov.-Dec. 2010

[5]   Kaufman, L.M.; , "Data Security in the World of Cloud Computing," *Security & Privacy, IEEE* , vol.7, no.4, pp.61-64, July-Aug. 2009

[6]   Lanjewar, U. A., & Rewatkar, L. R. (2012). Implementation of Cloud Computing on Web Application. *International Journal of Computer Applications* , 28-32.

Issues for Implementing ERP within Organisations

Vimal Patel

Department of Computing and Mathematics
University of Derby
Derbyshire, United Kingdom
Email: 100195301@unimail.derby.ac.uk

Abstract—The study critically investigates the critical management issues/barriers that resist the ERP implementation within organisations. Although ERP systems were introduced in the companies as a solution to various organisation problems and to further obtain an integrated infrastructure. Studies suggest that much of the issues in ERP implementation are from the user resistance and the strategies that need formulating in combating, this user resistance and most of it are the POST-ERP implementation when users begin to use the system. The core elements for this resistance are also identified as the lack of training, education, user expectations and finally the use of technology. The study will also focus on considering modern and emerging ERP technologies such as Cloud computing as an alternative small and medium organisation where cost is a constraint.

Keywords- ERP implementation, Cloud computing, ERP systems failures.

INTRODUCTION

"ERP is not a project; it is a way of life. ERP does not change anything, however the organization has to change the way of working" (Davenport, 1998). ERP systems aims in integrating set of software development within the organisation to share data among various functional departments which includes procurement, manufacturing, material, management, human resources (depending on the size of the organisation). According to Ibrahim (2010) ERP implementation is comprised of six major stages and is expected to consume few months to years sometime, the last stage being the POST ERP implementation. From the planning to the implementation is involved a lot of planning and consultation.

It is true that three quarters of the ERP projects are considered as failures and have ended catastrophically. Research indicates that the majority of failure factors are the research factor which is to implementation factors of ERP. It is arguable true that the major barrier in ERP implementation is from the people within the organisation contributing to 62% before the ERP go-live and is the figures are the same in the POST-ERP implementation.

According to Holland and Light ERP implementation will aim in the below benefits on the organisation (Holland and Light, 1999)
Provide solutions to legacy systems
- Reduce risk in development (Kelly et al., 1999)
- Business efficiency
- Increase global competitiveness (Markus and Tanis,1999)

It also poses drawbacks such as:
- Complexity in implementing (Martin, 1998)
- Problems associated with integration (Linthicum, 1999)
- High cost and late projects (Davenport, 1998)
- Resistance to change and organisational change (Sumner, 1999)

The research will therefore consider the systems failures followed by the data collection from various geographical locations to understand the ERP implementation failure trends in these regions and three stage methodologies is employed as the problem solution.

- The initial part examines the definition and importance of ERP in the organist ion and the need for ERP
- The second section will aim in analyzing the ERP system failure and mainly due to the ERP implementation within the organisation
- The third section will essentially assess the emerging ERP technology: *"Cloud computing"* and its contribution to ERP and finally, the last segment, provides theoretical perspectives on its implementation: the focus will be on the Unified Theory of Acceptance and Use of Technology Factors affecting technology implementation in organisations

ENTERPRISE RESOURCE PLANNING

Enterprise Resources Planning is a system within the organisation that seeks to ensure that its resources are carefully managed in order to give a good performance to its activities (Schafermeyer and Rosenkranz 2008). For the large organisations, this system is extremely relevant as it supports its functions and departments hence allow the organisation to face some of its challenges.

According to Aleke, Ojiako, and Wainwright (2011), and Schafermeyer and Rosenkranz (2008), ERP is important in that it allows the organisation to; first, identity its major functions and key resources, plan how to organize these, prepare an inventory of its main activities, establish the right resources for a given task (Rainer, and Turban, 2008). However, Scherer, (2005), cautioned against making the system or information technology to be one of the key resources within the organisation. This is because; organisations should be able to function without much dependence on information systems.

ERP SYSTEMS FAUILURE

It is estimated that 96.4% (Rao, 2000) of the implemented ERPs fail and 70% of implemented ERPs do not achieve the anticipated benefits (Al-Mashari, 2000). This has resulted in pushing the organisations to collaborate with external vendors/consultants to assist in adapting ERP systems.
Another predominant failure to ERP systems are the discrepancies in the approach and cost overruns and delays in the project are quite severe between the consultants and the organisation that could be another issue with ERP implementation (Motsios, 1999)

TABLE IX.   USER RESISTANCE EXPLANATION (SHANG & SU 2004)

Reasons of Resistance	Explanation
Parochial self-interest:	Resisting change to prevent losing something of value
Misunderstanding and lack of trust	Misconceptions about the implications and insufficient information of the benefits and gains
Different assessment:	Employees see more costs than benefits and those initiating the change see the reverse as true
Low tolerance for change:	Fear of not sufficiently developing the skills and behavior required
Increased efforts:	Additional efforts or abilities needed for the job

Further to it, resistance from employees are often causing serious barriers in the way of ERP implementation and it is true that nearly half of the ERP implementation is said to fail to meet expectation solely due to the underestimation in change management (Stefanou, 2000). Other underlying issues with ERP could be the conflict in the business strategy (Lionsky, 1995). This non-flexible nature pushes the organisation to fit the package and complicates their way of conducting business. It is arguably true that due to this, companies such as Foxmayer have led to bankruptcy (Davenport, 1998).

TABLE X.   RESULTS FOR MANAGGERIAL PROBLEMS DURING AND AFTER ERP IMPLEMENTATION

Type of Problem	Percentage
Project Cost Overruns	66%
Project Delays	58%
Conflicts with business strategy	42%
Employees Resistance to Change	42%
Conflicts with Consultants	38%
Internal Conflicts	34%
Conflicts with Vendors	30%

CLOUD – EMERGING TECHNOLOGY

A look at the importance of the emerging technology within an organisation also reveals that in many organisations, the choice of the system might depend on the costs and functional capabilities of the system (Aleke, Ojiako, and Wainwright 2011; Sharma et al, 2010). Emerging technologies like Cloud computing are viewed as systems that bears not major implementation costs on users and therefore, for any organisation, these are systems that can support cost reduction in two different manners; first the organisations can reduce its costs of operations in terms of using technology and secondly an organisation can reduce its costs through lack of investment on the new technology (Scherer, 2005; Sharma et al, 2010). It is therefore crucial to understand the idea behind the 'Cloud'. According to Burger, and Buskens, (2009), Cloud computing unlike many other emerging technology, does not depend on system being at the users premises (Aleke, 2006; Sharma et al, 2010). The vendor of systems will keep them and apportion some of the functions of the system to the organisation. While this has been coined as a revolution in facilitating access to technology, Scherer, (2005), and Scherer, (2004), noted that such a technology is not sustainable in the long run. The reason given for this is that when an organisation seeks to implement ERP, through the 'Cloud', it must decide between its most important resource (information) and the system. For large organisations the stake is even higher because, these organisations depend on the information that they gather for running their departments and therefore, cloud technology may not provide the best support to facilitate effective management of the resources of the organisation (Aleke, Ojiako, and Wainwright 2011). According to Oz (2006), and O'Brien, (2003), while Cloud computing is important and good for facilitating organisational development, its features and capabilities are always shrouded in uncertainty and therefore its implementation is essentially flawed.

VII.   TECHNOLOGY ADAPTION

In terms of the theoretical aspects of ERP implementation, the views by Vanketesh et al (2003), supports the notion that an organisation must carefully evaluate its positions vis-à-vis its need for the system before adopting the same. Such an evaluation must be done alongside existing needs within the organisation. These are essentially the externalities which can act as triggers and barriers to technology adoption (O'Brien, 2003). Two of the main barriers or triggers (cost and security of information) have been looked at in the previous section. The other factors might include the level of competition, access to the system, ability to implement the system within the entire organisation, the regulatory mechanism by the government, the speed of implementation desired and even the costs anticipated benefits (Burger, and Buskens, 2009).

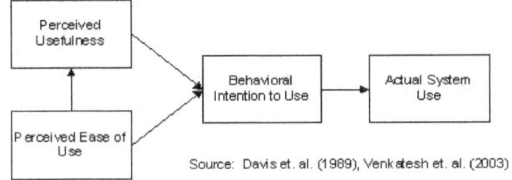

FIGURE I TAM MODEL DAVIS ET. AL. (1989), VENKATESH ET. AL (2003)

The Unified Theory of Acceptance and Use of Technology states that organisations must carefully evaluate its needs and factors external to its operations which might necessitate or hinder its ability to implement the new system (ERP). Implementation of ERP that is based on a new technology therefore provides the organisation with the right way of managing its information. However, while Cloud computing has this capability, Cloud computing falls short of supporting the organisation fully because, being an emerging technology, (Stair, Reynolds,. and Reynolds,2009), noted that it is not yet understood and therefore most organisations view such technology with a lot of suspicion. The need to develop robust systems whose functions and capabilities are known is therefore very important.

CONCLUSION

The paper has made attempts in critically understand the need for ERP within organisations and its benefits in particular. Whilst the benefits there also existed drawbacks not within the ERP system, but within the user group who had resistance in implementing the system. Three state analysis methods were deployed to seek the ERP need in the organisations through data collection from various locations and it is prominent that most of the critical issues are originated from the users followed by the project management effectiveness. From the study the outcome is on the ERP failures are mainly due to the managerial problems that are gathered in Table 1. It is noted that few organisations have failed and met bankruptcy due to non-flexible business strategies. The last and not the least user resistance and they contribute to nearly half of the discrepancies (Motsios, 1999). Whilst Cloud computing being a new form of technology can be of great benefit to the organisation, however, such technology are often viewed by many organisations are technologies that 'rob' organisations of its control over its information (Webb, and Schlemmer, 2008; Aleke, Ojiako, and Wainwright 2011). In this study, the need for creating an enabling environment within the organisation is paramount (O'Brien, 2003). Organisations must be in a position to carefully assess their needs for technology and the parameters needed to implement the same.

ACKNOWLEDGMENT

I am sincerely thankful to all the faculty member of Business, Computing and Law who directly or indirectly supported me during this article. I believe it is a great honour for me to be thankful to Richard Hill, Head of Subject of Computing and Mathematics who provided me with guidance to complete this article.

REFERENCES

[1] Aleke, B. (2010), Developing a Model for Information and Communication Technology Diffusion among Small and Medium sized Agribusiness Enterprises in Southeast 27 Nigeria, Unpublished PhD Thesis, University of Northumbria, Newcastle upon Tyne, UK.

[2] Aleke, B., Ojiako, U., and Wainwright, D. W. (2011) 'ICT adoption in developing countries: perspectives from small-scale agribusinesses', Journal of Enterprise Information Management, 24 (1), pp. 68-84.

[3] Alter, S. (2010) The Work System Method: Connecting People, Processes, and IT for Business Results. Works System Press, CA

[4] Beynon-Davies P. (2009). The 'language' of informatics: the nature of information systems. International Journal of Information Management. 29(2). 92-103

[5] Burger, M., and Buskens, V. (2009), "Social context and network formation: An experimental study", Social Networks, Vol.31 No. 1 (January), pp. 63-75.

[6] Davenport, T.H. (1998): Putting the enterprise into the enterprise system, Harvard Business Review, Vol.76 No.4, pp.121-132

[7] Farndale, E., Hope-Hailey, V. and Kelliher, C. (2011) High commitment performance management: the roles of justice and trust, Volume: 40 Issue: 1 2011

[8] Ibrahim A.M.A (2010): What organizations should know about enterprise resource planning(ERP) system Faculty of economics, Sebha university, Libya

[9] Motsios, T. 1999. 'Implementing ERP systems', Athens University of Economics and Business, Athens.O'Brien, J A. (2003). Introduction to information systems: essentials for the e-business enterprise. McGraw-Hill, Boston, MA

[10] Oz, E., (2006), Management information systems, Cengage Learning, USA

[11] Rainer, K. R. and Turban, E., (2008) Introduction to Information Systems, John Wiley and Sons, 2008

[12] Rao, S. S. 2000. 'Enterprise Resource Planning: Business Needs and Technologies', Industrial Management & Data Systems, 100(2): 81-88.

[13] Schafermeyer M., and Rosenkranz C., (2008), Inhibiting factors for adopting enterprise systems in networks of small and medium sized enterprises – an exploratory case study. Johann Wolfgang Goethe University. Germany.

[14] Scherer, M. J. (2004), Connecting to Learn: Educational and Assistive Technology for People with Disabilities, Washington, DC: American Psychological Association (APA) Books

[15] Scherer, M. J. (2005), Living in the State of Stuck, Fourth Edition, Cambridge, MA: Brookline Books.

[16] Sharma et al, (2010) Scope of Cloud computing for SMEs in India. Journal of Computing. Vol 2. Issue 5. Allahabad.

[17] Stair, R. M., Reynolds, G. and Reynolds, W. G., (2009), Principles of Information Systems, Cengage Learning, USA

[18] Shang,S. and Su,T. (2004): Managing user resistance in enterprise system implementations, Proceedings of the Tenth Americas Conference on Information Systems, New York, NewYork, August 2004

[19] Venkatesh, V. (2000), "Determinants of perceived ease of use: Integrating control, intrinsic motivation, and emotion into the technology acceptance model", Information systems research, 11, pp. 342–365

[20] Venkatesh, V. et al (2003), "User acceptance of information technology: Toward a unified view", MIS Quarterly 27(3): 425–478

[21] Webb, B and Schlemmer, F., (2008), Information technology and competitive advantage in small firms, Taylor & Francis.